Little Coin, Much Care: Or How Poor Men Live

Mary Botham Howitt

·LITTLE COIN, MUCH CARE:

OR,

HOW POOR MEN LIVE.

A TALE FOR YOUNG PERSONS.

BY MARY·HOWITT,

AUTHOR OF " WHO SHALL BE GREATEST ?" " STRIVE AND THRIVE,"
" SOWING AND REAPING," " WHICH IS THE WISER !" ETC.

NEW YORK:

D. APPLETON & COMPANY, 200 BROADWAY.

MDCCCXLII.

CONTENTS.

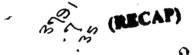

LITTLE COIN, MUCH CARE:

OR,

HOW POOR MEN LIVE.

CHAPTER I.

HOW MR. BARTRAM LET TWO OF HIS HOUSES, AND WHAT SORT OF TENANTS HE HAD.

IT just wanted five days to Lady-day, and Mr. Bartram, a fat little cabinet-maker, and the proprietor of the whole of Bartram's Court, Nottingham, was sitting in his small counting-house, at the back of his shop, reckoning up the amount which he had received of his weekly rents; for, it being Monday, he had just come in from receiving, or rather, we should say, from endeavouring to receive them. He was in an ill-humour, as he always was on such occasions; for, times then not being bad, and scarcely anybody out of work, he had, nevertheless, found more excuses than money, and that was a circumstance which would have irritated a temper much more placid than our Mr. Bartram's. Besides this, he had found two panes of glass, in the upper windows of No. 6, which had stood vacant all winter, broken since the last week, and the scraper gone from No. 7, which was untenanted likewise; and nobody could or would give any account of the depredators. It was a very provoking thing, said Mr. Bartram to himself, to have one's property thus destroyed; and a very strange thing, too, that tenants never feel so much regard for a land-

he thought his tenants were glad when any mischief was done; the people at No. 5 and No. 8 really looked so. He declared, with himself, that tenants made landlords hard-hearted; for, if there was a thankless, good-for-nothing set of people, it was poor tenants. Mr. Bartram next began to wonder whenever No. 6 and No. 7 would get let. The one house had stood vacant since Michaelmas last, and the other since Christmas. If, continued he, again falling into his argumentative vein, there was one kind of property which paid worse interest than another, it was small houses: he wished he could raise his rents, to indemnify himself for losses of all kinds; and then he ran over in his mind all the extraordinary conveniences and advantages of these same houses, which he himself had built, whose hobby they were while building, and to which he had given his own name. Did not every house consist of five good rooms, say nothing of the lean-to behind, which served as a scullery, and which was furnished with a good stone sink, where all washing and slopping might be done, and thus leave the kitchen as sweet and clean as a palace? say nothing of the lean-to, nor of the nice little well-shelved pantry under the stairs, were there not four good rooms fit for any respectable family to live in? What a pretty kitchen it was, with its good range, its oven and boiler, and a well-built dust-pipe behind, to keep all neat and tidy; a pretty mantelshelf above, and a nice corner-cupboard! Then, too, the two bed-rooms above, so light and airy, with the walls stencilled in such pretty patterns, the one buff and the other blue. True, the stairs were a little narrow; but what of that? poor people never were very fat: then there was the attic above, which, though somewhat in the roof, was as good a room as he himself would desire to sleep in, with a fire-place and all, and weather-tight in the roof, which was more than most people could say about attics!

There was no doubt about it, reasoned Mr. Bartram; he was a very ill-used man, and had the most ungrateful set of tenants of any landlord in the town; but you need never look for gratitude, said he, from the poor: make a place as nice as you would, they never thanked you, but would go and live in narrow, little, nasty holes just as willingly as in the most airy and the most convenient. Why, was there not a pump in the middle of the court, which he had always kept in repair, and the sinking of whose well had cost him unknown money? and yet, after all, these two houses seemed as if they could find no tenant, and there was scarcely a house besides vacant in the whole town! Of course we are writing of the prosperous times in Nottingham: not many years afterwards, Mr. Bartram, and many another landlord besides, had to lament over whole courts and streets of vacant houses.

Mr. Bartram struck his fist upon his desk, in the energy of his dissatisfaction, and was just about falling into a second soliloquy, when he was interrupted by the appearance of a woman, apparently about thirty years of age, decently dressed in a dark printed gown, a faded cotton shawl, and a bonnet; which, from its old crape and peculiar form, told her at once to be a widow. She walked straight through the large furniture-shop with a determined step and air, as if she very well knew the business she came upon entitled her to all privileges of the place; knocked at the glass door of the counting-house, and then, without waiting for Mr. Bartram's permission to enter, walked in.

Mr. Bartram had, as we said, just struck his fist upon his desk, and found the thread of his musings suddenly broken by this visitor, whose knock he had not heard. She was a large-featured, sallow-complexioned woman, with a cold eye and a hard expression of countenance; there was something repulsive about her; and, though it was evident she was a widow, compassion was never an observer's sentiment towards her.

Without apologizing to Mr. Bartram for the interruption or intrusion which her sudden presence might be considered by him, she saluted him with a "good even-

ing," in a very business-like manner, and said she
wanted the key of No. 6, which she wished to see, as
she thought of becoming its tenant. Of all things Mr.
Bartram wanted a tenant for No. 6; but, someway or
other, he felt displeased by her cavalier manner.

"Why did she not go there in the morning," he
asked, "when she must have known that he was there?"

"I have my own business of a morning to attend
to," said she, "without thinking what time your business takes you into the court, and must have the key
now, or not at all!"

Mr. Bartram felt more vexed than ever. "What
was she?" he asked. "A woman that could maintain
herself and her children reputably, and pay her rent
honestly," she replied, in a tone of determination rather
than displeasure.

Had Mr. Bartram been agent for the houses in this
court, instead of their landlord, it is very likely he would
have quarrelled with the woman; but, as proprietor,
he remembered that No. 6 had stood vacant since
Michaelmas; so he meant only to stand out a little, as
any landlord might do, which only makes a tenant more
eager. So, without reaching her the key, which hung
on the wall opposite to him, just above his desk, he
said, that No. 7 was also at liberty; but in the first
place, who was she? was she a Nottingham woman?
and where did she live?

"Either yes or no," replied she; "can I have the
key of No. 6? No. 7 I do not want. I have no time
to stand shilly-shallying here; and, as to who I am, and
what I am, why, bless the Lord! I am as honest and
respectable a woman as any in Nottingham!"

Mr. Bartram began to think, from her manner, that
if he offended her he might perhaps lose a respectable
tenant; so he reached her the key, and said he would
follow her in about a quarter of an hour.

"You need not trouble yourself about that," said she;
"I shall not run away with your key. I wash at Mr.
Tomkinson's the bookseller to-morrow, and will bring

it myself. You can know my character from Mrs. Tomkinson; or Mrs. Parker, on the Pavement; or Mrs. Buchan, or Mrs. Lacey, in Castle Gate; I am Mrs. Higgins, the washerwoman, and you need be afraid neither for your key nor your rent!" So saying, she folded her arms in her shawl, and, bidding him good-night, as if she quite expected him to take her at her word, went out.

Mr. Bartram followed her through the shop, and then stood with his hands in his pockets, looking for some time through his shop-window. He had not stood long there before he began to apprehend that a very respectably dressed man and his wife, who seemed to be in deep conversation together, had an intention of coming into his shop. A shopkeeper soon learns to detect a customer, even at the distance of half a street, or a wide market-place. Mr. Bartram's best customers were the working-class; and his warerooms above stairs were full of bedsteads, clock-cases, chests of drawers, tables, and looking-glasses, made to suit their tastes; for, in those days, lace-weavers, stocking-weavers, and artisans of all kinds, got good wages, and lived prosperously; eating and drinking of the best, and buying whatever article of furniture pleased their fancy, often without knowing to what purpose to put it, or where it could stand in their crowded houses.

Most respectable, decent looking people, were this couple; and Mr. Bartram felt quite prepossessed in their favour, feeling sure that almost immediately he should be in his warerooms above, recommending, as he so well knew how, the various articles of his trade. The man carried a baby in his arms, and she was holding a little fat child, of perhaps three years old, by the hand.

" You can go in, John," said she, " and just ask what the rent is, and whether we can have the key; and I'll take the baby."

" But you'll go in too?" said the husband, giving the baby into her arms.

" Nonsense!" said she, " what should I go in for?—
that's Mr. Bartram himself in the shop!"   The man
thought it *was* nonsense that he should want his wife
to go with him, when he only needed to ask a simple
question; so he turned the handle of the shop-door at
once, while his wife, with the two children, went saun-
tering past the shop-window.

Mr. Bartram was better pleased that it was the key
of No. 7 that they wanted, even than furniture; the
demand for that, he thought, would come most likely
afterwards.   He was all at once in a most excellent
humour.   He thought it was a fine thing to be a landlord, even with vacant houses to let; and especially so,
as this new applicant, unlike the former, treated him
with deference and respect.

Mr. Bartram gave the key, with a little bow, meant
to be very polite: saying, that he himself was going
down to the court this evening, and would join them
there.   He had, he said, an applicant there for another
vacant house, and must go on her account: he had, he
said, only two vacant houses, and they were both in
demand: it was always the case, he added, with his
houses, for people readily found out what was good
and cheap.

Without being asked the question, the new tenant
elect said that his name was Ford; that he was a lace-
hand by trade, and now lived in New Snenton, but
that he wished to take a better house; that he knew a
fellow-workman, Jones, who lived in Bartram's Court;
and he and his wife liked Jones's house so well, and as
the water was so plentiful and so good, they wished to
move there.   Mr. Bartram, although, considering the
temper in which Mr. Ford was, it was hardly necessary,
said a deal in praise of his houses; a deal in praise of
the pump in the middle of the yard; and a deal in
praise of himself, as landlord; to all of which the other
responded with the utmost complacency; all which
occupied so much time, that Mrs. Ford, who had
passed and repassed the shop several times, and had

seen the key, from the very beginning, between her husband's fingers, began to be quite impatient at the delay.

Mr. Bartram and Mr. Ford at length came together to the door; and then the latter, seeing his wife, remembered that she was waiting; so, saying " Good bye" to the landlord elect, joined her, took the baby again in his arms, and they all walked across the market-place as briskly as the fat little legs of the three-years old child would allow.

Mrs. Higgins, the washerwoman, was turning the key in No. 6, as the Fords turned the key in No. 7. They thought she was a very unpleasant looking woman; and Mrs. Ford remarked, that, although she was a widow, she was sure she should never like her as a neighbour.

The two new tenants came into Nos. 6 and 7 on the same day. The two broken panes of No. 6 had been repaired, and the missing scraper of No. 7 replaced; both houses had been white-washed, and blue-washed, and yellow-washed, and thoroughly cleaned within and without. There was not a pin to choose between the two; the only difference was, that the door of one house opened in the right-hand corner of the kitchen, that of the other in the left, the chimneys of both houses running up between the two.

Mrs. Higgins' furniture came at twice, in a hand-cart. A large cart, drawn by a strong horse, brought the Fords', besides sundry baskets-full of small and frangible articles, which were carried in the hand. Both families were, of course, very busy during the greater part of that day. Ford was there himself, in his shirt-sleeves, carrying in, arranging, and helping his wife; and, besides the two children we spoke of as accompanying them to Mr. Bartram's shop, there came now three elder ones; a boy of ten or twelve years old, and two girls, each a year or so younger; these, if they did not assist much, were quite as active as their parents. A bee-hive in full work on a July morning

never looked busier than did this No. 7, Bartram's
Court, on the day when the Fords came into it. What
a many hands and arms were stretched out to carry
everything portable from the cart to the house! what
bustling and striving and laughing there was, to get
broad and heavy things in at the door; and still more,
to get them up the narrow staircase; and withal, what
care was taken that no wire in the top of a bed-post,
no corner of a table or chest of drawers, should scratch
or injure the newly-washed and newly-stencilled walls;
and what delight it was to the children to see into all
the well-filled drawers, that were taken out of the
chests to lighten them, and now stood piled up one
across the other on the house floor. "Oh! look,
Jane, here's your new frock!" said the brother; and
"Look, John, that's mother's best shawl!" and "I
wonder whatever that is wrapped up in the paper; I
should not wonder if it's something very pretty. I'll
just tear a little bit of paper off, and look!" It was a
very pleasant thing this flitting, the children thought;
and the father and mother seemed to think so also, for
they never seemed in better humour all their lives
than then.

How comfortable No. 7 looked by the time it got
dusk! The chaos was then, in a great measure,
reduced to order, the horse and cart gone from the
door, and all swept up, within and without, giving, at
once, an earnest of the well-to-do, orderly sort of
people who were come to reside there. John, the
elder boy of the family, was the only one at all dis-
contented with the family arrangements; he, poor lad,
had to sleep by himself in the attic, which, let Mr.
Bartram say what he would, had but very little to
recommend it. The girls were delighted with their
bed-room, with its tent-bed with blue checked hangings, and its chest of drawers, containing the more
valuable wearing apparel of the family; together with
the papered trunk, in which their own common clothes
were kept. But their bedroom was nothing to that

of their parents; they thought that quite sumptuous!
What a goodly show that excellent four-post bed
made, with its gay chintz hangings; beside which
stood a crib for the baby; just, for all the world,
thought good Mrs. Ford, like anything in a gentleman's house. There were three chairs and a wash-
hand stand and towel-horse set beside it; for Mrs.
Ford prided herself on knowing how things ought to
be; so, though she and her husband and children
were mostly washed in the scullery below, and the
ewer was not very regularly supplied with water, yet
there they stood, looking very neat and proper; and
there was the dressing-table, also, with a white frilled
cover, and a very good looking-glass standing upon it,
which said looking-glass was very regularly used, both
by Ford and his wife; for they, like all people, be
they rich or poor, who have any desire to dress well—
and very natural it is, too—wish to see themselves
when they are dressed. Besides these articles of
furniture, there were two bedside carpets, and half-a-
dozen gay scriptural prints, coloured and glazed, which
had been bought by Ford, before his marriage, at the
great annual fair. There was Adam and Eve in
Paradise, The Death of Abel, Abraham sending forth
Hagar, Abraham offering Isaac, Joseph sold by his
Brethren, and Boaz and Ruth; beautiful pictures these,
thought the young couple, as they admired them on
the walls of their first kitchen, and which were now
only removed to a chamber, to give place to four
larger ones, which Ford, at the instigation of his wife,
had bought only lately at the sale of an old family's
furniture.

The house of the Fords was exactly that of a prosperous Nottingham lace-hand about the year 20 of this
century; consequently, therefore, interminable would
be the inventory of all that the lower room or kitchen
contained. There were well made chairs, with and
without arms, all comfortably cushioned; there was a
second-hand mahogany dining-table as good as new, set

against the wall, covered with a new green cloth, with
a printed yellow border; there was a very fine mahogany chest of drawers with a secretary top; a handsome clock in a case, as good as money could buy;
two workboxes, one of rosewood, which belonged to
Mrs. Ford; and another covered with red morocco, be-
longing to her eldest daughter; together with a tor-
toiseshell tea-caddy, with a glass sugar-basin inside;
all of which stood upon the secretary; while a looking-glass in a gilt frame slanted forward over the dining-
table, upon which were laid a large Bible and Prayer-
book, and about a dozen different works taken in by
Ford in numbers—Philip Quarl, Henry Earl of More-
land, Cook's Voyages, The Young Man's Instructor,
Universal History, Complete Herbal, and such like.
On each side the glass hung one of the large engravings;
another over the secretary, facing the window, and the
fourth, which for some time seemed a supernumerary,
over the door.   White dimity curtains, duly fringed,
clothed the window, and a muslin blind forbade the
inspection of impertinent neighbours.   Three or four
toasting-forks, one of which only was ever used, a bot-
tle-brush, a red japanned hearth-brush and bellows,
and dozens of articles of bright tin and copper and
brass, and even some plated, hung in the corners near
the fireplace.   On the mantelpiece above were ranged
brass candlesticks, in the centre of which stood a
bright copper tea-kettle; and smoothing irons of all
kinds, with box and Italian, seemed to balance either
end; whilst on a neat rack, which was hung to the
ceiling, were laid a flitch and a half of bacon; and two
hams, in white paper bags, hung on the staircase, lest
they should grease the walls of this goodly-conditioned
kitchen.

Never, surely, was there so comfortable a poor man's
kitchen as this.   Ford, however, could not be called
a poor man.   He was sober and industrious; but his
money came too freely for him to know its worth.
Like many another man in those days, he earned several

pounds a week, all which vanished nobody knew how. His wife in many respects resembled him; she had a pleasure in spending. They certainly were very happy people; they both of them had known hardships in their earlier years, but they knew none now. Theirs was a house without care, without even the care of saving money.

It was with uncommon pleasure, we may believe, that Ford and his wife surveyed their new house towards evening, when a great deal of all the necessary bustle of arrangement was over, and things began to look in order. They thought it was the nicest place they had ever seen; and Mrs. Ford could not help wondering aloud, as she had wondered to herself many times in the course of the day, what sort of people they were in the next house, and what sort of furniture they had brought with them; for both she and her husband had a sort of contempt for people who had not good furniture, and who, to use their own phrase, did not keep themselves and their children smart and nice. She looked upon the room and all that it contained with the greatest complacency, and, drawing a round table to the hearth, broke up the fire, which, beginning to sparkle and blaze, made the kettle sing out merrily, and cast a warm, cheerful glow over everything, like a good-humoured smile upon a human face. Jane set the tea-things on the little round tray, and began to cut slices of bread, which John kneeled down upon the hearth to toast; when, all at once, a bitter cry was heard from the next house, as from a child being beaten.

"Oh, gracious goodness!" exclaimed Mrs. Ford, setting down the teapot, into which she was just about to pour boiling water, "that mother is beating her child." The young Fords all looked uneasy, as the child in the next house continued to cry, and blows, accompanied by a hard, threatening voice, were painfully audible.

"The woman's a brute," said Ford, running with the

c

baby in his arms, and opening the door, whilst the mother felt sick, as if the sufferings of the child entered her very heart: she said she should not eat a morsel that night.

Presently all was still; and Ford, who had gone out towards the window of No. 6, came slowly in again. " Well, what can you see?" asked his wife, who met him at the door.

" Nothing," said he, in a tone of apparent indifference, and shut the door behind him. Mrs. Ford said she wished their chimneys were not adjoining, for that they should hear all that went forward in the house; and nothing made her so ill as to hear children misused. She listened with her ear almost within the chimney, but all was silent; so she poured the boiling water into the pot, and setting the fat child on a tall chair beside the table, prepared the tea, and then took the baby, that her husband might have his meal in comfort.

" And now," said Ford, after he had seen his wife thoroughly enjoying her tea and toast, " I will tell you something."

Mrs. Ford looked up from the knot which she was untying in the baby's pinafore.

" It was a cripple, that that woman in the next house was beating," said he.

" Oh, Lord!" exclaimed his wife, " and a child too?"

The children said, eagerly, that they had that morning seen a poor little hump-backed girl coming with a crutch after the hand-cart that brought the goods; that she looked very tired and miserable, and was very ugly besides. " Poor little wretch!" said the mother, in a tone of such compassionate sympathy, that both children felt at once a sentiment of the tenderest humanity towards their unhappy and ill-favoured little neighbour.

Next morning Mrs. Ford went to the pump for water, and, as she came back, a girl of ten or eleven years old leaned against the door-post of No. 6, with her hands behind her, balancing herself on one leg. She seemed one of those pert children, cunning, sly, and unabashed, who are more knowing than their years. She wore a faded printed frock, a black stuff apron, a yellow glass necklace, and had her hair twisted up in papers all over her head, with small rings in her ears. She nodded very familiarly to Mrs. Ford, and bade her good morning.

"Good morning," replied Mrs. Ford, and went into her own house.

Before long, she saw the girl peeping in at one corner of the window, where a corner of the muslin blind happened to be turned up; and presently afterwards she came boldly in, with a cup in her hand.

"Can you lend us a bit of sugar?" said she, "for mother's gone out and has locked up everything, and there's no sugar, not even a bit for our pudding."

"Does your mother often go out?" asked Mrs. Ford.

"Yes," said the girl, "every day, only Fridays and Saturdays and Sundays: she goes out washing. She washes for everybody genteel in the town, and gets plenty of money, only she's very stingy; she always locks up eyerything besides what she leaves us to eat. She says she's very poor, but I know she's plenty of money; I wish I'd as much, that I do!"

"But if your mother goes out and leaves you in this way, you'll be setting the house on fire, or doing some mischief," said Mrs. Ford, fearing that themselves and their good furniture were endangered by such neighbours.

"Bless you!" said the girl, "we have no fire; I wish we had. When we lived in Leicester we lived in lodgings, and so we did till we came here, and then we had a bit of fire in a morning; now mother means to take lodgers herself, and then we shall have fire again, and go to school too."

"And why do you not go to school now?" asked Mrs. Ford.

" I don't know," said the girl, " unless it's too far.
We used to live at Hyson Green, and go to school there;
but that's too far for Letty."

" Who is Letty?" inquired Mrs. Ford.

" My sister," replied she; " she's so lame, she can't
walk, and she is so cross and so disagreeable, I hate to
be left with her! she can't play, and she gets into such
passions you don't know!"

" Was it Letty that was crying last night?" asked
Mrs. Ford, " and that your mother was beating so?"

" She deserved it," said the girl; " she would not get
out of the way, and she made me drop the salt-box,
and spill all the salt, and it fell, salt and all, into a tub
of water; and I was so vexed, because I had some
sugar screwed up in a paper among the salt: a good
thing, however, for me, for if mother had found the
sugar, she would have beaten me too."

" But you were a very naughty, unkind girl," said
Mrs. Ford, " to let your poor lame sister be beaten because you spilled the salt."

Jemima, or Mima, as her mother called her—Miss
Higgins, as she called herself—took up the cup, which
Mrs. Ford had filled with sugar, and went out, saying
to herself, with a toss of the head, that the lady at
No. 7 was a very disagreeable set-up sort of body, and
she would now go and see whether they were good
for anything at No. 5.

CHAPTER II.

HOW MRS. HIGGINS LET HER ROOMS, AND WHAT SORT OF LODGERS SHE HAD.

TILL Mrs. Higgins came into Bartram's Court, she
had lived, as her daughter said, in lodgings; but now
she intended to take lodgers herself. Accordingly,
within three days after she had settled herself in her
new abode, a written paper, pasted at the entrance of

the court, announced that two or three good rooms
were to be let at No. 6; and a fellow paper in the
window of the said No. 6, intimated that any one
desirous of taking such rooms, must apply within; and
and Mima, or Miss Higgins, in the absence of her
mother, was empowered to give necessary, or at least
preliminary information respecting them.

Had Mrs. Higgins been satisfied with the first appli-
cants who presented themselves, she might soon have
let her rooms; but, in the first place, the rooms were
unfurnished; for she required that the lodger should
bring furniture as a guarantee for his rent; and more-
over, she looked for other qualities and qualifications
from her inmates, namely—that they should take upon
themselves, during her days of weekly absence, a
general oversight of the lower room, which, with the
lean-to, was all that she occupied. She had but little
furniture—no more, as we said, than a hand-cart brought
at twice, and everything that could be secured, was
carefully kept under lock and key; but what little
there was, required, as she said, looking after. Her
lodger, therefore, must be some bonnet-maker, or
dress-maker, or a stay-at-home person of some sort or
other, who, on consideration of the low rent at which
she offered her rooms, would just see that the children
did not set themselves on fire in a morning before they
went to school; where, taking their dinner with them,
they remained all the day; and also keep the key
inside the door till her return home at night.

Mrs. Higgins was not a woman to stop short in the
full accomplishment of any scheme, because of difficulty, or even temporary disappointment. It was her
boast, that when once she set her mind on a thing,
she did it. Spite, therefore, of all that her neighbours
said to the contrary, after about six months, and after
about a dozen trials of so many different sets of
lodgers, she found herself admirably well suited in a
very decent elderly couple, without family, who took
up their abode with her. The man had been, for

c 2

many years, the driver of one of the Pickford vans, and was away from home the greater part of every week, and every Monday and Thursday mornings went to the van office at three o'clock; so that, on those mornings, his larum woke her, and her fire warmed his coffee. Nothing in the world could be more convenient.

The wife, who was slightly troubled with an asthmatic complaint, never went one step further out of doors than she could help; once a week to the market, and once a week to the nearest church; and that on Saturday and Sunday, two of the days when Mrs. Higgins was home. Thus, she was the most desirable inmate that could be conceived.

All other lodgers, within the first few days, had quarrelled with Mrs. Higgins; but Mrs. Greaseley, who was the quietest person in the world, quarrelled with nobody. Like everybody else, she disliked her landlady; but, as she never went out gossipping with her neighbours, she kept her sentiments to herself; and Mrs. Higgins fortunately being out so much, they got on very well together. She cooked her little piece of meat three times a week, in Mrs. Higgins' oven, very scrupulously bringing down each day a lump of coal, as an equivalent for the service done; and, if she found it difficult to tolerate the pertness of Miss Higgins, the mother's favourite, her kind heart was touched with sympathy for Letty, the poor cripple, who, ill-used both by mother and sister, was humbly grateful to be permitted to take refuge in the chamber of the gentle-spirited lodger.

Not a morning, however, passed, without her having to interfere between these ill-paired sisters. Poor Letty was peevish and suspicious; Mima overbearing and selfish. Mima was always the first ready for school, and then persecuted her feeble sister with threats and upbraidings. It was in vain that the lodger remonstrated; Mima was incorrigible; and all that could be done was to expedite the lame girl, and then watch them out together across the court; after which, Mrs. Greasely hoped, but by no means felt sure, that they would go on amicably together.

Weeks and months passed on; and Mrs. Higgins, as she said, washed for all the genteel families in the town. According to her account, and according, also, to the account of her employers, there was no such washerwoman as her to be met with. She told her lodger, that if she had ten pair of hands, and could divide herself into ten different bodies, she should have more washing to do than she could get through. There was but very little furniture in Mrs. Higgins' two rooms, if room the lean-to might be called, which, with its one bed, served them all three for chamber; still, the little that they contained was as carefully kept as Mrs. Ford's superabundance. On Friday, she invariably washed at home; on Saturday morning, cleaned up her rooms and all that they contained; and on Saturday afternoon, ironed and mended the clothes. Wretched days were these for poor Letty, if it chanced to be wet, so that she could not go to school; for her mother had no patience, and, apparently, no affection for her. All her life long had she been an infirm, helpless being, and now, at ten years old, was of stunted, dwarfish growth, with shoulders of melancholy deformity, and so lame in one hip as only to walk, and that painfully, by help of crutches. The severity and unkindness which she had experienced through her life, had made her peevish and irritable; whilst the contrast between her treatment and that of her sister, which every act of her mother's behaviour made her bitterly sensible of, fostered in her heart a secret feeling of envy, not to say malice. And let not our young readers think with prejudice against poor Letty, from this cause: she was deformed in person, and pitiably plain in feature, with every probability of growing deformed in mind also; not from any peculiar tendency to evil, but because coldness,

not to say unkindness, had repressed all her ten-
dencies towards good.

Letty never knew what indulgence and forbearance
were, till she knew Mrs. Greaseley. It is true that
Mrs. Ford was filled with kindly compassion towards
her, from the evening of their first neighbourhood,
when she heard her suffering from the blows of her
mother; but Mrs. Ford, good woman as she was, was
too much prejudiced against Mrs. Higgins to interfere
about the child. She did it once or twice; and each
time she and her neighbour quarrelled violently:
besides this, poor Mrs. Ford, who prided herself on
the good looks, well-grown forms, and hearty good
tempers of her children, had hardly more patience
with poor Letty's petulance than her mother; so she
contented herself with calling the one " that poor
little wretch!" and the other " that horrid brute!"
and, after Letty seemed cared for by the kind-hearted
lodger, troubled herself no further about her.

Letty's greatest delight was to go into Mrs. Greasely's
room, and look through the large bag in which she
kept her patchwork, all so neat and tidy, with the
different little bundles of printed cotton sorted in
their different colours. For four years, at least, Mrs.
Greaseley had been engaged over one very elaborate
quilt: she only worked at it now and then, as a piece
of indulgence, and never too long at a time, that the
pleasure might not pall. When she worked at it, she
allowed Letty sometimes to help her; and even when
she was not at work, permitted her to turn over the
bag which held the unused store of patches.

Letty found it very entertaining, and would amuse
herself for hours with pretending that somebody
had said she might choose a new frock for herself,
and that she had now, therefore, the agreeable task
of choosing the very prettiest from all these pretty
prints; neither did she admire with less devotion than
Mrs. Greaseley herself, the new quilt in progress, with
all its stars and roses set so daintily upon their white
ground.

Mrs. Greaseley had in her rooms many little chests
and boxes, all of which she kept carefully locked. She
carried a great bunch of keys in her pocket; and when
she wanted anything from any of these locked-up
places, she only opened the lid half way, or drew out
a drawer just so far as to allow what she wanted to be
taken out, as if they all contained great treasures, which
she was very unwilling any eyes should see. Mrs.
Higgins did just the same. Letty supposed it was the
way with everybody who had keys and locked-up
places. Her mother locked up everything below
stairs, and carried her keys in her pocket, just like
Mrs. Greaseley.

Letty was the most inexperienced and ignorant
child in the world, and all this locking up and mystery
excited her imagination mightily. What would she
not have given to have examined, through and through,
the desk which stood in their kitchen, and which was
above the drawers that contained the family clothes!
She had but very few clothes herself, she knew—they
did not fill half a drawer. What could her mother
have in all the other four, and in that great chest
which stood in the lean-to, beside their bed? but above
all, what did that desk contain? She had once had a
glimpse into it; had seen a many little drawers, and a
little arched doorway in the middle, and above it
other little drawers. She had seen her mother once,
when a servant from one of the families where she
washed, came to drink tea with her, take some silver
spoons from one of the drawers: it was altogether a
memorable day, which she was never likely to forget,
for they had muffins to tea, and mutton-chops, cherry-
pie, and a bottle of wine for supper, which the servant,
whom Letty thought so very goodnatured, said she
must share equally with them. This glimpse into the
desk gave Letty a half-defined sort of notion that her
mother had a deal of valuable treasure contained there.
She did not know, herself, what kind of treasure; for
she had, as we said before, no experience of anything.

She was much too lame to walk far, and had only once in her life, and that was when they came here, gone through the town from one end to the other. The market-place seemed to her a vast and splendid world, and its shops the most splendid that could be conceived. Once, and only once, she had been to the fair; how her mother came to take her there, she could never tell; and that once she would never forget. The dancing-booths, the shows of wild-beasts, the bazaars, with all their display of trinkets and toys—what a wonderful region of enchantment it was! She forgot that she was lame; she forgot that everybody said that she was a little ugly thing; she forgot her mother; she forgot Mima, as she stood surveying all the imagined treasures around her; and now, though it was two whole years since, she remembered it as the bright spot of her existence. She fancied that desk of her mother's like a booth in the fair; and Mima said she knew all that was within it, and that Letty believed; for her sister's yellow glass necklace, the very first time she saw it, had been produced from that desk. Poor Letty had far more curiosity than her remote ancestress Eve, it was a passion which might be almost called a disease; and when she thought of that desk, with its mysterious interior full of little drawers, and doorways leading to and containing unimaginable things, she became almost feverish with impatience and curiosity. How often she plotted little schemes with herself, of how, if ever she could get her mother's keys, she would make an excuse to stay from school, and, all alone, become mistress of these mysterious secrets.

For many months the poor child had satisfied herself with ransacking the lodger's patchwork-bag; but every pleasure palls with the using, and, in time, she was obliged to confess to herself, that the bag was too familiar; every bundle of prints she knew, as it were, by heart; she could not even cheat herself into a belief of their novelty.

" Oh, if I might just see what is in that box !" said
she, one day, as she sate with the patchwork-bag on her
knee, into which she had no desire to look, and fixing
her eyes on a little old black walnut chest, which stood
on a stand in a corner, and from which Mrs. Greasley,
who had been taking something, was just removing her
keys.   Mrs. Greaseley very often went to this box; it
seemed to contain a world of things; and Letty's
curiosity had been excited by it for months.

" You must mind and lose nothing out of it, then,"
said her good-natured friend.   So, leaving the bunch
of keys still in the lock, she set it down upon a chair.
Letty sate on a wooden footstool, and, almost breath-
less with delight and expectation, looked first at Mrs.
Greaseley, and then at the box; so astonished was she
to find her wishes so readily fulfilled.   There was a
looking-glass inside the lid, which made it very heavy.
Mrs. Greaseley said Letty must take care, or the lid
would fall back and break the hinges, or the glass, because the tapes which supported the lid were broken.
She said she always held it in her hand, and did not
open it wide on that account.   Letty thought if there
was a looking-glass in the lid of her mother's chest in
the lean-to, how large and grand it must be, and how
much she should like to see it !

There were many winders of bright-coloured silks
in the box, which Mrs. Greaseley told her she had had
many, many years, ever since she was a girl and worked
embroidery at school on white satin, which was afterwards framed, and even now hung, as Letty might
see, in her bedroom.   Letty went to look.   " Was it
that bunch of flowers, tied together with ribbon, that
now looked all so faded ?" asked she.

" Yes," replied her friend; and then went into a
long history of all the work she had done at school;
how she had sprigged a white linen gown with blue
and yellow cruels, far more beautiful than any print
that ever was;—she said Letty would find a piece of
it somewhere.

Letty did not listen very attentively to all that the old lodger said, because she was busied with the contents of the box. Besides the winders of ancient silks, she found reels of modern cotton, balls of worsted, a pair or two of scissors, and a piece of scarlet cloth, on which were stuck the good housewife's store of needles. All these were things of inferior interest; but then came a layer of curious antique ribbons, of various colours and patterns, several of them woven with threads of gold and silver. To every one of these was a history attached;—this had belonged to her mother; this to her great aunt; this had been given to her by her godmother, and that by one of two old maiden ladies, with whom she had lived in a long servitude, and about whom she would, she said, some day, tell Letty a great deal. Letty had in her hand at that moment a little housewife, made of gold brocade, a most beautiful and curious little thing, which would have excited the desires of any collector of antiquities. "It was two hundred years old, at least," said Mrs. Greaseley, "and had belonged to a great duchess, an aunt of the ladies with whom she had lived. Letty must open it," she said, seeing her look so long on the outside, as if she hesitated to undo its little silver clasp. When it was opened, nothing could exceed her amazement; the gold brocade looked so bright and new, and the bunch of flowers, that was wove in so fresh and beautiful!—she could tell every flower, as if it were natural. Then there were little pockets, lined with green velvet; and flaps of scarlet cloth for needles, bound with gold thread; still more than this, there was a looking-glass, and a little pair of scissors, now, however, rusted. Mrs. Greaseley said there used to be a knife, bodkins, and tweezers also; but that, someway or other, they had got lost. She said, she was very fond of this housewife, and set great store by it; she believed people who bought curiosities would give a deal of money for it, but that she never meant to sell it. It must have been an hour before Letty was satisfied with

looking at it; she never, in all her life, had seen anything so beautiful; it exceeded whatever she had imagined of the possessions of kings and queens. She no·
longer wondered now at Mrs. Greaseley opening the
box-lid but a very little way.

Next she took out a straw bodkin-case, and then a
straw pincushion; they had been made, her friend said,
by French prisoners, during the war. Letty thought
them very pretty, but they did not occupy her long:
next came an old red leather housewife, which, Mrs.
Greaseley said, she must be very careful in opening,
as it contained many things which she valued. Letty
took great care in opening it; there were within,
many little flapped-down pockets; she was greatly
disappointed, however, in their contents. In one was
a quantity of different coloured sewing silks; a finely
cut watchpaper in another; in a third, a little old yellow paper case, containing court-plaister; and, in a
fourth, a quantity of very light curling hair, wrapped
in paper. Mrs. Greaseley sighed deeply when Letty
showed it to her. She said it was the hair of her only
son—of the only child she ever had; that he was
drowned when he was only four years old, and that it
was a sorrow, she believed, she should never overcome. The poor woman would have talked for hours
of her boy, if Letty had listened; but though she paid
attention for awhile, she became impatient, and, having
fastened again the red leather housewife, into which
her friend had very carefully put the light, curling
hair, and taken out further sundry small articles, she
exclaimed, with surprise, that that was all! and yet
the box itself was not half empty; it was not half so
deep inside as it seemed without.

Mrs. Greaseley then touched a spring at one corner,
and, the front of the box falling down, revealed two
little drawers. Mystery within mystery! what a
delight was this to Letty!

" It is a very old-fashioned box," said her friend;
"they do not make such now-a-days."

It looked so like the inside of her mother's desk, that Letty was overjoyed. In the first drawer she found half a dozen silver tea-spoons and two salt-spoons, a broken silver knife, and three or four pair of wrist-buttons, of Bristol stones, set in silver, and a piece of cut glass, full of angles, through which Mrs. Grease-ley told Letty to look, that she might see how pretty it was, especially when she looked through it at the light. Letty was in raptures; it gave her ideas of jewels, and diamonds, and all kinds of precious things. She sate looking through it for a long time; Mrs. Greaseley said that her poor little boy found that piece of glass in the street, and that he took the greatest possible delight in looking through it; she said it looked prettier still by candlelight, and that, some night, Letty should see it.

These things were contained in the upper drawer; the lower one was fastened. Mrs. Greaseley said it was her husband's drawer, and that he kept the key of it; one of his watches was kept there, and his money, and nobody, she said, went to it but himself.

" If I could only just for once see into this little drawer," said Letty, " I never would ask you again."

Mrs. Greaseley was the kindest creature in the world, and her heart was just then particularly tender, by thinking of her lost child; perhaps, also, he might have taken the same delight in prying into locked-up places as this poor lame girl; however that might be, without saying another word, she took up the bunch of keys, which she had laid down on the table when she opened the front of the box, and, unlocking a drawer in a chest of drawers which stood in the room, drew out her husband's Sunday waistcoat, from the pocket of which she took a small ring, on which was hung a watch-key, and a little common key; with this she opened the drawer, saying, at the same time, that it contained nothing worth seeing.

Letty's eyes were twice their usual size, as she peered into the opening drawer. The first thing she saw was a large silver watch. "It was his brother's watch," said Mrs. Greaseley; "it is a very good one; he likes it much better than his own, but. he does not often wear it."

She wound it up with the key that hung upon the ring, that Letty might hear it tick; and then she opened it, that she might see all the little wheels and works inside. Here again was a delight! she looked up in Mrs. Greaseley's face and thanked her, almost with tears in her eyes, for showing anything so pretty, and so wonderful.

"Did you never see the inside of a watch before ?" asked the lodger. She said she never had; that she had often wondered what was inside a watch, and had wished she might have one in her hand; that there was one which hung over her fire-place in their school, but she never dared to touch it. Mrs. Greaseley let her hold this in her hand, and she thought to herself what rich people the Greaseley's must be, to have so many valuable things. It was a full half-hour before she was satisfied with contemplating the watch.

After awhile, however, curiosity got the better of surprise and delight, and then she was impatient to know what further remained to be seen. Mrs. Greaseley came to her side instantly, and said there was nothing farther for her to see; there was nothing besides in the drawer but a little bag—a bag made of leather, in which her husband kept his money; "she would not open it," continued she, " even for the king; for that, if she did, he would be very angry." Letty asked, " had she never, in all her life, looked into that bag ?" " Yes," she replied, "she had done so sometimes, but only when her husband was present; he was a very exact man, and very particular about his money, and she should not wonder at his knowing if anybody touched it."

So saying, she put the watch again into the drawer, locked it, and then replaced the key in the waistcoat-pocket, as before.

It was an hour or two before Letty had put everything back again into its place, many things having to
be again and again examined, with even more wonder
and delight than at first.   The box was tenfold interesting to her, now that she knew how singular was its
construction, and how interesting its contents.   She
asked Mrs. Greaseley if she had ever seen large boxes
made in that way, with drawers under them.   Her
friend replied, that sometimes there were double bot-
toms to large chests, within which things were kept
secretly.   Letty, from this time, did not doubt but
there must be a double bottom to her mother's large
chest in the lean-to; and she thought, time after time,
" Oh that I could but get the keys, and see all the
strange and beautiful things that mother keeps locked
up there !"

CHAPTER III.
HOW THINGS WENT ON AT THE FORDS'.

A LONG time after this, Mr. Bartram told some of his
acquaintance, that of all his eight-and-forty tenants he
had but two that he could call respectable; only two
who were worth anything; only two who, every Monday morning when he collected his rents, had the
money ready for him; only two who looked upon him
as anything better than a street-robber, though, heaven
knew that there was not a better landlord than himself in all the five wards of the town; and, odd enough,
he went on to say, these two tenants lived in adjoining
houses, and, which was odder still, came into these
houses on one and the same day.   He declared that it
was a pleasure, any time, to go into No. 6 and No. 7;
they were sweet and clean as a posy on a May
morning.   He could sit down on a chair there, without
any detriment to his clothes; and it always did his

heart good only to see the red bricks of the floor, and the bright glass of the windows. He said, he held them up each week as examples to all the other forty-six of his tenants; but, someway or other, it never did any good—poor people would not be taught: he said they were as stupid as asses, and it was his opinion that there was not one person in the whole court who liked either the Fords or Mrs. Higgins, for this simple reason—that they were the only respectable people in it.

Mr. Bartram went on expatiating on the want of principle and gratitude in poor tenants; it was a favourite subject with him. A deal that he said was very true, although he dealt in common-places: he said, that however much money they got, they were never the better for it, because it was "slatterned" away in trifles, that did them no good. He said, that if the lower classes were at that time poor and in distress, when the lace-trade was so brisk, and artisans who made frames, and weavers who worked in them, could earn so much money, what would their case be when this prosperous state of things came to an end, as the wisest heads and the most far-seeing people expected it soon would? He, as the landlord of poor tenants, he continued to say, should have to suffer equally with them; whilst in one thing, however, he said, they had a great advantage over him: they never looked forward to any change; they had no fearful anticipations of evils to come; they expected that, because they had plenty now, plenty would last always; they were just like the dumb animals in the field, that in summer time trample down far more than they eat, nor look forward to winter, when the richest pasture is frost-bitten, and bare as the dreariest common.

Mr. Bartram fancied himself very eloquent and philosophical: he spouted at political clubs, and wrote letters for the newspapers, on the state and prospects of the working-classes; but with all this, he produced very little effect upon his six-and-forty tenants; so he set them down as " incurables."

It was now two years since the Fords became dwellers in Bartram's Court. The house looked as clean and bright as it did on that first evening, when Ford and his wife, with their children, sat down to tea; and the fire-light glimmered and shone on the looking-glass and the four pictures, and on all the polished brass and tin ware, which decorated the walls. The good mahogany clock-case, and the chests of drawers, and the dining-table, and the nice round table, stood there, as then. Nothing had been pawned; nothing had been sold, but many things had been bought in fresh, till the house, which we thought full enough at first, was now literally crammed with its contents. If the furniture could have spoken, what an outcry would have been heard among it, for want of elbow-room!

Ford had exchanged his old silver watch for a good repeater; his wife had a new work-box, a new tea-caddy, a new set of china tea-things, and jugs of all patterns and sizes, and wine-glasses, and even two decanters, in red japanned stands; together with several new gowns, one of silk, and a new shawl, " a real lady's shawl," the shopman assured her, which cost two guineas. Above stairs, there were considerable additions also; new bedsteads, and new chests of drawers—for their family in the meantime had increased also. Whatever Mr. Bartram might say, and that justly, of the Fords' respectability and regularity of payment, not a word did they deserve on the score of providence.

Of the Fords there were now six children. John had now gone to school these several years, and was, everybody said, a good scholar; he had, however, grown pale and thin. His mother said, so much learning did not agree with him, so she used very often to give him a holiday, and send him out into the meadows to run about, and bring, as she said, a little of colour into his

pale face, which, she declared, made her quite ashamed
of him, lest people should think he had not enough
to eat.

Jane, the tidy little housewife, at "the time of the
flitting," was as tidy, and far more useful now than
then. She, too, had gone to school, but it was not for
reading and writing that she got praise; she was, as the
school-mistress said "no great hand at either one or
the other;" the praise that she won was for needlework.
What neat, regular, back-stitching she performed !—
what excellent button-holes she made! how quickly
and well would she dispatch a long seam ! She could
knit also, and net. She had netted her mother a cap,
and herself a little scarf, and for the house a pair of
stout window-blinds. She could mark; she had worked
a sampler, and was now busied on a pair of worsted-
worked footstools. Jane had her mother's talent and
genius, as it were, in her fingers; whatever the hand of
either had to do was well done.

The second daughter, Rachel, a gay, giddy girl,
made acquaintance with all the neighbours' children,
and even was found with a blue necklace of Mima
Higgins' in her pocket, which she had borrowed to
wear one Sunday, when she walked out in the meadows; and, very much to the vexation of the mother
and elder sister, was continually getting up little inti-
macies with the most disreputable girls in the neighbourhood. The three-years-old child, at the time of
the flitting, had since then died, had died of the hoop-
ing cough in the winter—the only trouble the Ford
family had experienced since they came. The child
that was then " the baby" of the family, was now the
" little Stephen," fat, and rosy, and good tempered,
the most beautiful child, Mrs. Ford thought, in the
world, with dark brown, curling hair, and brown eyes,
full of kindness and love. Stephen was "the baby"
for three years, and then a successor took his place,
" the last of the flock," and was now three months old.

Jane loved her brother extremely, but she was of a

temperament very different to his, buoyant and hopeful; nothing ever depressed her. He, on the contrary,
was somewhat reserved and shy, thoughtful, and of a
sedentary turn. He loved all his family, but Jane the
most. He, boy as he was, saw wonderful beauty in
her rosy cheeks, and large bright eyes. She, with
sound health, both morally and physically, loved all
the household; she would have said she had not a pre-
ference among them, but everybody could see that
little Stephen was her favourite; her mother told her
so often; she said Stephen was everybody's favourite.
Did not Mrs. Greaseley give him bread-and-butter and
sugar? and did not Mrs. Higgins herself blow bubbles
for him from her wash-tub? and if Mrs. Higgins, whom
everybody disliked so, and whom, everybody said, had
such a bad heart, did so, was it not a proof how much
love little Stephen won; and then she would clasp her
arms round his fat, white neck, and kiss him till his
rosy cheeks were redder than roses.

They were a very happy family, these Fords. Everybody said, it seemed as if no trouble could ever come
near them. They were a happy and a prosperous
family, although, it must be confessed, that Ford, now
and then, spent part of his wages in liquor; yet it was
only now and then. Everybody called him a sober
man; his family never knew what want was, and, as he
was so good-tempered when in liquor, what did it matter? It would be so different if he came home storm-
ing and out of humour with them all, as most men did!
There was not a wife in Bartram's Court that did not
wish her husband such a one as Ford.

The day after a carouse, Ford was always as low-
spirited as he had been elevated at the time. He
lost his own self-respect, and was impatient of his own
weakness. He made the most solemn vows never to
be over-persuaded again; but again and again, time
after time, good company, as he called it, made him
find how vain are mere vows. By degrees, his wife
became conscious of a little anxiety, lest this weakness

should become confirmed habit; it was but a little anxiety as yet, for Mrs. Ford was not what is called " a croaking person." She still called herself a happy woman," but she began to look, " both before and after," more than she had ever done as yet; and the more she did so, the more dissatisfied with herself, and the more anxious she became. There is scarcely a human being who does not find it so with himself.

It was a fine balmy afternoon, at the end of March; birds were singing in the tall trees behind the court; all the streets of the town were becoming dry, and everywhere children were out at play, some in the streets themselves, and others were gone abroad with little brothers and sisters, and neighbours' children, whole companies of them, into those beautiful meadows which stretch between the town and the river Trent, and which, at that time, were lilac over, with the abundant bloom of the lovely spring crocus. Throughout the town, everywhere—at door-sills and within the street itself—lay scattered hundreds of these flowers, which had already been gathered; and yet, hundreds and thousands and millions of them remained, and sprang up every day for their gathering. The children of the Fords' were out in these same meadows, with a basket, to gather these flowers. They were all out—the baby and all: the baby and Stephen drawn by their elder brother or sister, in a little carriage, cushioned with pillows, and wrapped up as warm as if they lay in bed.

Mrs. Ford sat at her work, trimming a straw bonnet with blue ribbons; two others, already trimmed with different coloured ribbons, stood on the dining-table, on those little light stands used in bonnet-makers' shops. Mrs. Ford had taken, the last summer, to cleaning and turning straw bonnets, and even to making up bonnets of silk. She had never served an apprenticeship to the business, but she understood it as if by instinct. She attempted it as it were by accident, and then, finding her success complete, con-

tinued it, not only for profit but pleasure. She was
becoming rather famous in her own neighbourhood,
particularly among servants in respectable families, for
the pretty, genteel way in which, they said, she
trimmed bonnets. It was very easy to her: the
ribbon in her fingers seemed to fold and twist itself
elegantly; a bow, without labour, and almost, as it
seemed, without thought, took instantly a pretty form,
when she designed to make one. Had she been
trained to it, she would have made a first-rate milliner:
she thought so herself, and had just become conscious
of a little ambition. She began to aspire to a shop—
a pretty little shop, with a nice bow window filled with
supports, each holding a bonnet ready trimmed, or,
with suggestion for a trimming, in form of a blue, or
green, or red ribbon, placed lightly across it. She
felt, instantly, that she knew so well how to arrange
these things, and make them look pretty and attractive.
She thought over all the bonnet-makers' shops in the
town: she thought, suppose that the largest of them all
belonged to her; and suppose that ladies drove up to
her door in their carriages, tried on her bonnets, and
gave their orders; suppose that she had half-a-dozen
smart young women, in black silk aprons, sitting at
work in a back parlour that opened into her shop by a
glass door; suppose that she went to London twice a
year, as the great milliners did, and brought down the
fashions with her, and then sent out neat little printed
notes, which said that—" Mrs. Ford, grateful for all
the favours she had already received, informed the
ladies of Nottingham and its vicinity, that she had
received her spring fashions; and that a new and
tasteful assortment of bonnets and caps would be ready
for their inspection, on Monday, the 29th instant, to
which she respectfully solicited their attention."

Something like this, Mrs. Ford knew, was the
accustomed style of a bonnet-maker's and milliner's
circular, and she grew warm in contemplating the ideal
greatness which she had called up before her. She

sighed, however, the moment afterwards, in thinking
how much money such an establishment as this must
require; and that generally, people, as the saying is,
creep, and then go. She thought, then, of neat little
unexpensive shops at the corners of streets—merely
the front room of a small house with a bow window,
put in, perhaps, at the expense of the tenant, ambitious
of becoming a tradesman, or tradeswoman. She thought
of such in Wheeler Gate, and in small streets leading to the
market-place and park, which were thoroughfares, and
which yet would not be very expensive; and the more
she thought, the less of folly or of impracticability there
appeared in the idea. She had often, before this afternoon, cultivated the scheme. She had, even last
summer, mentioned it to her husband. She began to
think, that if they then had rigorously began to save,
they might, perhaps, have had now ten or twenty
pounds in hand; and ten pounds in hand was a nice sum.
The more she reviewed in her mind the purchases she
had made since then, the more she regretted never
having thought of saving before; but it was so hard,
argued she, to resist spending money when one had it,
and when there was no immediate, or no important
object to be accomplished by saving. There was her
silk gown, which she had worn but once, and that at
the cherry-eating at Wilford, and which so provokingly
had got stained with a crushed cherry—how well the
might have done without that! and that fine scarlet
coat that she bought last winter for Stephen, he might
have done with one at half the price; and the baby
might have done with its hood quite well, even through
the summer, without her having laid out so much
money in its bonnet, although she made it herself.
She wished, too, she had not bought that new set of
tea-things, nor the new tea-tray; although everybody
said it was so cheap. She began to add up what she
might have had in hand had she saved even the cost
of these things: it was more than ten pounds! It
would be a long time before she could accumulate ten

pounds, were she to begin from that very day. She
wished her husband did not spend so much money in
drinking. Suppose it was true, as people said, that
before long the lace-trade would change, what a bad
thing it would be that Ford had a habit of drinking!
For the first time almost in her life she blamed him;
but, blaming him, she blamed herself also the next
moment for an equal disregard to the value of money.
What pleasure she had always had in seeing the house
nicely furnished, in seeing herself, her husband, and her
children neatly, and, for their station in life, perhaps,
expensively dressed. She resolved that henceforth
she would resist the desire to make purchases; she
would have to struggle, she knew, against her own
natural disposition, but still she felt sure, that with an
object like the one which now interested her, she could
overcome it. A good resolution is the first step to
right action, and Mrs. Ford felt pleased to have even
resolved well.

It had been her intention to buy the baby a new
frock, and Stephen a pair of new shoes, that very
evening, when she and her husband went to the market;
she had promised Jane that Stephen should have a
pair of red morocco shoes: it would disappoint Jane
sadly, and Stephen too, who had been that very day
bribed not to cry by the promise. His old shoes really
were not so bad, argued she now, in her new view of
things—not too bad even to be worn on a Sunday; and
as to the baby, it could do very well without anything
new, at least for several months.

She was determined to begin that very day to lay
up money. She would put a paper in her window, as
she did last summer, saying that bonnets there were
cleaned, and turned, and trimmed; and she would
add, " on the cheapest terms," which she had not
thought of before, but which she knew very well, even
to people with plenty of money in their pockets, was
often an inducement—often a bait; and also, when she
took home these three bonnets, she would ask the

persons to whom they belonged, to recommend her to
their friends.

What a pity it was, thought she, that their house was
in a court like this, where there was no passing, else
she would have asked Mr. Bartram to put them in a
bow window; and, considering what good, regular
tenants they had been, there was no doubt in the
world but he would have consented; or, even if he had
not, they might have done it at their own expense.
She began to be dissatisfied with Bartram's Court; she
wondered at their having stayed there so long. Almost
every house had changed its tenants unnumbered
times, excepting theirs, Mrs. Higgins's, and the Jones's.
Now, however, she determined to look out this very
evening, in every thoroughfare street through which
she passed, if there was a small likely house to let. At
all events, she would get her husband in the mind to
change before the next quarter; midsummer would be
a good time for the flitting; and, though people did not
want as many autumn and winter bonnets as spring
ones, still she did not fear but she should find demand
sufficient to make the change profitable.

Never did a castle in the air, however ambitious its
materials, seem more captivating to its builder than
did this of the smart little bonnet-shop, well situated
in a thoroughfare street, seem to the mind of poor
Mrs. Ford.

Just at this stage of her musings, she was somewhat
startled by the door suddenly opening, and by the
entrance of a man in a short jacket, half-boots, and hat
somewhat conceitedly set on one side of his head. He
touched his hat without removing it, and came side-
ways in at the door, smiling with a very familiar and
friendly face; and then Mrs. Ford recognised the
travelling dealer in japan-ware, from Birmingham,
from whom she had already, at various times, purchased so much. By this time his whole body was in
the house, together with a large package of tea-trays,
caddies, japanned jugs, and coffee-pots, which he car-

ried strung over his shoulder. He turned them off
from his back, as if he were shooting down a sack, and,
like one certain of a customer, took out his handkerchief, wiped his forehead, and said now he had got
something exactly to suit her taste.

Mrs. Ford, without rising from her chair, said she
was afraid, that day she should not become a purchaser.

" You will say differently, presently," said the man,
beginning to untie the green baize cover of his tea-
trays; " I know you will say differently, presently."

Mrs. Ford said it was no use; that she had bought a
tea-tray from him only the last time—and she glanced
at the one which was reared upon the dining-table,
and that she said she had not yet used.

The man still persisted in untying his package; and,
glancing, like her, at the tea-tray, said, " Yes, it is a
beautiful pattern—quite a papier-machée pattern, and
I have brought a second size to match it, on purpose."

Mrs. Ford shook her head, and the man, no whit
discouraged, presented the tray to her. She thought
how pretty it was; she thought, that, had it not been
for the shop scheme, it certainly would have tempted
her.

" Only three-and-sixpence," said he.

" I have not so much money in the house," said she,
really glad of the excuse; " I have only half-a-crown."

" I'll trust you the shilling, and ten times the shilling,"
said the man; " I shall be here again in three weeks.
Come, make it a sum worth trusting—buy this pretty
bread-basket—it will match it!"

" No," said Mrs. Ford, " I have no intention at all
of laying out any money to-day;" and, to give force to
her words, she went on with her bonnet.

" Come," said the man, coaxingly, " what shall I
tempt you with? You never sent me away before
without a purchase. I must not let you lose a good
habit; and, upon my word, I have not shown this
waiter to any one, because I meant it for you. You

shall have it for three shillings. Let me put it now,
where it ought to stand," added he, and reared it within
the larger tea-tray on the table. " How handsome it
looks! Only three shillings! or, rather than you should
not have it, I will say half-a-crown, and that's less
than I gave for it: it would cost you four-and-sixpence
in the shops!"

" I shall not buy it at any price," said Mrs. Ford,
calling up a very firm resolution to resist a temptation
which she felt to be strong.

" It's an offer," said the man, beginning to fear that
he should not succeed, " that I would not have made
to any one else. I wish you would buy it: to tell you
the truth, I want money; I have made but bad sales
this time in Nottingham: I want money very bad, and
I offer it dirt-cheap."

" I assure you," said Mrs. Ford, beginning, on her
part, heartily to wish him out of the house, " that I
have made up my mind to lay out no more money in
furniture of any kind; I have plenty—more than I
want; and we have a large family."

" Very good," said he, without taking the tray from
where he had placed it; " but perhaps you may want a
coffee-pot—that's always useful in a family. Here's a
good japanned coffee-can, far better than any Queen's
metal, or Britannia metal, or German silver, or Shef-
field plate—always sweet and clean, will cost you
nothing in plate-powder nor whitening, and will look
good to the last."

Mrs. Ford said that she had already bought such a
one from him.

" It will make me quite unhappy," said he, " to go
away, and sell you nothing!" and, putting one hand on
his hip, he stood for a moment, as if in consideration,
and then, suddenly beginning to untie a brown-paper
parcel, which he had carried in his hand when he
entered, and set down on the ground, he continued—
" You must buy something for those pretty children of
yours, if you'll buy nothing for yourself. Let me per-

suade you with this pretty drinking-can—a half-pint
measure at the same time—see, " A present for my
dear boy—for my dear girl, or for my good boy or
girl—which you like. Yours are all both good and
dear! Come, now, choose which you will!—well-made
and sound; will bear a blow, or may be knocked down
—only sixpence a-piece!"

Mrs. Ford thought of the shoes she had promised
Stephen. She had made up her mind not to buy them,
however; still, she knew all the time, that he would
be disappointed, and so would Jane: suppose she
were to buy him a can instead. The shoes would
have cost her two shillings—this only sixpence; she
should thus save one shilling and sixpence if she
bought the can: a promise was a promise, and ought
not to be broken, even to a child; but from this time
forth she determined not to promise what she might
afterwards find it advisable not to perform. It was
making a sort of compromise, both to Stephen and to
her own weakness; but in future she would not spend
a penny which might be spared. She accordingly put
her hand in her pocket, took the half-crown from the
red-leather purse, and, the man seeing her yield, made
a fresh attack in favour of the little tea-tray.

· Mrs. Ford was resolute; and he went away almost
angry, from his want of success, while she sate, for the
next half-hour, persuading herself that she had done
quite right; although she felt that, spite of her own
arguing, she would have been better pleased if she had
resisted altogether.

Stephen was overjoyed with his can: he said he
liked it far better than new shoes: Jane shook her
head, and looked greatly dissatisfied; and then, after
a search through her own and her mother's work-box,
found a piece of black ribbon, and sate down to bind
afresh the old shoes, that he might be fit to be seen,
she said, on Sunday.

CHAPTER IV.

MARKETTING AND DISAPPOINTMENT.

FORD did not come home, as usual, that night, to go with his wife to the market. It was a very singular circumstance. He worked for a master who paid his men at five o'clock on a Saturday, that they might have the opportunity, that evening, of laying out their money advantageously. Ford and his wife went regularly together to make their purchases.

She waited and waited till it got quite dark. The three bonnets were to be carried home; they were packed in a bonnet-box, and had now stood ready for two hours. She knew her husband would carry them for her, for the owners of the bonnets lived but very little out of the way. The baby was undressed, had been fed, and now lay asleep in the cradle; Stephen was in bed; Jane had got the children's things ready for Sunday, and had now sate down to practise braiding on a piece of nankeen, with green worsted braid. She wanted to braid a dress for little Stephen, and her mother had promised it her for a reward, if she would keep the childrens' stockings mended. She was very assiduous to deserve the reward, principally, it must be acknowledged, for the reward's sake. Rachel was threading glass beads for a necklace, and John was busied just within the scullery-door, that he might have the benefit of the kitchen-light, setting crocus roots, which he had brought from the meadows, in two flower-pots. He was very fond of flowers; these crocuses had an inexpressible charm for his mind; he fancied nobody loved them so well as he did. His mother told a story of him, when he was a child—that he had cried because his father walked among the flowers and crushed them. John did not know it himself, and nobody knew it either; but he was a poet in feeling—a born poet—although, as yet, he had never breathed a sentiment in rhyme.

E 2

Mrs. Ford put on her bonnet and cloak, for it was now half-past seven, and said John must go with her to market; though, as the father was not come home, there was but very little money to lay out; but she would go round with him with the bonnets, and, perhaps, somebody might pay for them, and thus they should be able to get enough for the present; and, perhaps, after all, they should meet the father by the way. So, bidding Jane and Rachel keep in the house, and take care that nothing was set fire to, she bade John take the bonnet-box, and, herself carrying the market-basket, they went out.

Mrs. Ford had two shillings in her pocket, and one of the servant-girls, whose bonnet was thus delivered, punctually paid half-a-crown which was due, admiring all the time, the pretty, tasteful way in which it was trimmed; and promising, as did the other two, who did not pay, to recommend her to all their acquaintance; who, they assured her, had plenty of bonnets to clean and trim.

Mrs. Ford, with the four-and-sixpence in her purse, and the market-basket in her hand, walked hastily along Bridlesmith Gate; for she was afraid that what was good for anything would be bought up before she got to the market; for, what with going round with the bonnets, and stopping a few minutes at each place to bespeak the patronage of her servant-friend, the Exchange clock had already sounded only one quarter to nine. She walked quickly, but not so quickly as to pass, unobserved, a new little bonnet-shop that had been opened that very morning, towards the market-place end of the street. She paused, impatient as she was, to look in at the window; the gas was burning brightly from two jets covered with glass shades; a dozen bonnets at least, some trimmed and others untrimmed, were in the window, more were on the counter, and three or four purchasers, almost filling the little shop, seemed quite willing to give the new establishment an earnest of their good wishes.

A middle-aged woman took one of the bonnets from the window; and Mrs. Ford saw that the proprietor of this new shop was no other than Mrs. Dunnett, who, only the last summer, began bonnet-making in Narrow Marsh. How could she have managed? Perhaps she had had a legacy left her; perhaps she had been a careful, saving woman all her life.

Mrs. Ford stood looking in at the shop-window, as if she were rivetted to the pavement. Mrs. Dunnet's daughter was sitting on a stool within the counter, trimming a bonnet, and Mr. Dunnet, he who was only the last year a lace-weaver, like her husband, was unpacking a case of leghorn-bonnets. Oh! sure enough, the Dunnets were steady, saving, industrious people—they had not, all these years, been spending their money for nothing! From some cause or other she felt all at once disheartened. But why so? She said to herself, that she would take courage—that, from this day forth, she would lay up every farthing which she could earn or save; that the children should work likewise, and learn, likewise, to save. For their sakes, as well as for her own, they would all imitate so good an example.

"Father!" exclaimed John, who, while his mother was looking in at the shop window, was noticing the people, who, coming and going, almost filled the narrow street, and among whom he suddenly recognised his father.

Mrs. Ford looked quickly in the direction in which her son had spoken, and saw her husband.

"John!" said she. He turned round quickly when he heard the voice, and joined them. His hat was a little on one side, his coat buttoned crookedly, and his countenance had that merry, somewhat foolish expression, peculiar to him when in liquor. His wife sighed deeply, for her mind was at that moment filled with ideas of care and prudence, and every species of economy: she did not, however, either reprove or

reproach him, but putting her arm within his, turned him
back towards the market-place.

"And now, where is your money?" said she, thinking
with herself that she would keep her own four-and-
sixpence as a nest egg, upon which to begin saving.

"What are you going to buy?" asked her husband.

"We must have a few pounds of meat," said she;
"we want potatoes, but we may manage, perhaps, till
Wednesday; but I have promised the children some
rhubarb for a pudding to-morrow, and, if it is not too
dear, we will take some: we must have a pound of
butter, two ounces of tea, half a pound of coffee, a
pound of candles, and half a pound of soap."

Ford clucked with his tongue within his mouth at
each enumeration of articles by his wife, as if he would
say he thought "she was doing things rarely!"

"Well, where's your money?" said she.

He put his hand deep down in, first one trowsers-
pocket and then the other, but no money came. He
then felt within his other pockets, but neither was
there money there. He stopped short, and the half-
silly expression of intoxication suddenly became one of
fuddled earnestness.

"Where in the world can it be?" said he, with
rapid impatience. He searched through all his
pockets, emptying their contents into the market-
basket.

"Good Heavens!" exclaimed his wife, in a tone of
dismay, "is it possible you can have lost it?"

Ford leaned against one of the pillars of the market-
place colonnade, and tried to collect his clouded
faculties. "It hardly was possible," he said, "that he
could have lost it." He appealed to his wife if he had
ever lost money before. She confessed that he had
not, to her knowledge; and then suggested that, as he
had been drinking, perhaps he had left it on the table,
or somewhere in the room; and said that they had
better at once go and inquire. She said this, because

she feared to trust her husband again in the room with his old companions, in the state he then was.

Ford, who believed himself now completely sober, said that she and John should just make such purchases as were absolutely necessary—that was, if she had any money with her—which he did not doubt, said he, laughing, for she always had money.

"For God's sake! John," said she, holding him firmly by the arm, "drink no more to-night—you have already had too much!"

"No," said Ford, "I will not touch a single drop—you may depend upon it—not a single drop." He quite intended to keep his word; and, despairing of ever finding his money again, went back to the Sir Isaac Newton, which was the public-house his comrades were accustomed to frequent, and where he had spent the evening; where, unfortunately, he found again the same set of "good fellows," as they called themselves, whom, an hour before, he had left, all now in a state of high carouse.

Mrs. Ford, as one may imagine, made no expensive purchases that night; her marketting was soon done. There was a very small piece of meat, and that not a costly joint, bought for the Sunday's dinner; but no rhubarb at all for a pudding; nor was there butter, nor tea, nor coffee; for she was determined, that if her husband's money was quite lost, they should, as a family penance, none of them drink tea or coffee that week.

"John," said she to her son, as, on their return, they repassed Mrs. Dunnett's new bonnet-shop, and she saw them all still busy in it, "I want to have a little talk with you. You are a very good scholar, John, and, for your years, a very thoughtful, good boy; I'll tell you now what I want to do, and in what way I think you can be of use to me."

John linked his arm into his mother's, and, spite of the noise and bustle that surrounded them, listened attentively to every word she said. He was pleased to think that his mother considered him worthy of trust.

"I want to begin bonnet-making on a larger scale," said she, "I want to have a shop, and be able to lay by some money for our old age, and to set you all up in business of some sort or other. There's Mrs. Dunnett, that used to live in Narrow Marsh, and last summer used her kitchen as her bonnet-shop, just as I might do, has now opened a pretty shop in Bridlesmith Gate. It will take a great deal of money, though," continued she, "and we must save all that ever we can. What do you say, John, to beginning to work in the frame? You know you are a big boy now, and have had a deal of schooling."

John, poor fellow, in his inmost mind did not at all like the idea of working in the frame, and, surprised by this announcement of his mother's wishes, if not intentions, walked on in silence.

"You know, John," continued she, attributing his silence to a child's natural disinclination to work, "people who would get on at all in the world, must not fold their hands together, and expect meat to drop into their mouths. My father used to say the same thing to us children: we thought him a very unkind father; perhaps he was a little too severe with his children, but he was right so far as never to let any of us be idle. Had he lived out his days, he would have left some little money among his children; but, unfortunately, coming home one foggy winter's night from market, he missed his road on a field-foot-path, and walked into a stone quarry, and was dashed to pieces."

Mrs. Ford fell into a musing of some minutes, which her son interrupted by inquiring if his grandfather was a sober man?

"Quite sober," replied his mother; "he never let his wife or children drink anything but water. I was only thirteen when he met with his death. My mother took a rheumatic fever; she was, poor thing, a bad manager, and everything fell into confusion after my father was gone. We were soon.so poor that we had not bread to eat. My grandfather took my mother home to his house: he was a poor man himself, and we children went out to service. I know what poverty is, John," continued she—" you do not. I know what it is to long for a dry crust of bread, or a cold potato—to go to sleep ravenously hungry —to dream of eating all night long, and then to wake with sickly pangs, as if at my very heart. Please God! my children shall never know what the hunger of poverty is." Mrs. Ford's voice quivered as she spoke the last words; and John, who was not used to see his mother affected to tears, but with a soul filled with every tender sentiment, and capable of every noble emotion, felt as if suddenly grown older in experience—as if conscious of responsibility laid upon him, and of the noble capability of self-sacrifice.

"Mother," said he, clasping her arm within his own, "I will work—I will do all that ever I can to help you!"

His mother's tears flowed down apace; she was excited by many things that night; and when she entered the house, the first exclamation of the two girls was, " What's the matter with you, mother?—why, you have been crying, and so has John!"

John said that his father had lost all his money; that, perhaps, somebody had picked his pockets; and that he was now gone back about it; and that their mother could only buy very little for them to eat, and there would be no rhubarb pudding for the next day.

" Oh, never trouble yourself about there not being enough to eat," said Jane; " we can eat anything: but I am sorry about the rhubarb. Poor little Stephen," said she, " I told him about the rhubarb pudding when he went to bed—I am so sorry; and he is not to have his shoes either!"

" Go to bed, children; go to bed!" said Mrs. Ford, in a tone of decision very unusual to her.

" Must I go too?" said John. " I want to sit with you till my father comes home."

" No, child, no!" said his mother; "your father will not be long, and I would much rather be alone."

The girls went to bed dissatisfied, and so did John, who felt as if his mother had refused his sympathy—had thrust him back again from her confidence.

Mrs. Ford, without taking the things from the market-basket—without taking off either her bonnet or shawl, sate down and began to think. She felt as if the spirit of her father were come over her; as if she could pass severe judgment, both upon herself and her husband; as if, even towards the children, she could act sternly. She and her husband had been weakly lavish: they had let go, perhaps for ever, the golden opportunity of reaping a harvest by economy; they might begin to save now, but it would take years to redeem the past.

As to the children, they must work; she was grieved to think they were not like the Higgins's; she did not often quote Mrs. Higgins as an example for herself, but in this instance she did. "There's Mima has worked at mending three years almost—why cannot our Rachel do the same? and Letty, the poor little cripple, she has her frame at home, and earns, I am sure, more than she consumes. I have been blind indeed," thought she, "never to think of these things before. Yes, yes, the children must work." John, she decided should go to the frame, and Jane she would instruct in the straw-bonnet business, that, whenever she was able to have a straw-bonnet shop like Mrs. Dunnett's, her daughter might be her assistant. As to her husband, she must excite him to take an interest in her plans. He was easily beguiled into liquor, she knew, but he was too sincerely attached to her and the children to become a reckless drunkard; he was such a different man to Jones, who had fallen by degrees into habits of regular drunkenness, and now brought home no money at all to his family; he was so different to any other married man in the whole court.

She began at length to grow quite impatient for his return. How long he had been! why, really it was almost twelve. Surely, surely, thought she, they have not over-persuaded him again. She then thought of Mr. Dunnett unpacking the case of Leghorn bonnets; and it seemed to her, that *he* must be removed from all temptation. He had parted company, as it were, with his old lace-weaving associates, and, far in advance of them, was ascending up the hill of independence and fortune; and, before his death, would have placed his family in the class of respectable tradespeople! " I will see my husband in the same position," said she; " who knows but there was a time, even when Mrs. Dunnett herself sate scheming as I do now?"

As she sate pondering thus, with the fire dead out, and the unsnuffed wick of the candle grown almost into an extinguisher, she was startled from her reverie by the house-door being tried. She started up to unfasten it, knowing it must be her husband. It was two watchmen, who had brought him in; he had fallen in the street, they said. Mrs. Ford inquired, almost frantically, if he were hurt?

" No," said they, " he was only in liquor. He was quite dead-drunk, and they thought they had better carry him to bed."

Jane started up aghast, when she saw two men carrying her father through her chamber to his; and John, who slept in the garret, and had been woke also, half dressed himself, and stole down to see what was the matter.

" Your father has drank too much," said the mother, with a deep sigh. " Go to bed, and go to sleep also, for it is long past midnight."

Instead of going to bed herself, however, when she had fastened the door after the departed watchmen, she quietly put by her purchases, made all straight and neat for the Sunday, and, as there was no fire, and

F

the night was cold, she laid a woollen shawl over the baby in the cradle, wrapped herself in her cloak, tied a handkerchief over her head, and sate down to sleep in the kitchen armed chair.

CHAPTER V.

HOW TWO PEOPLE CANNOT ALWAYS THINK ALIKE AT FIRST, YET HOW IN THE END THEY MAY.

TRUE to her determination, herself and the children breakfasted on milk and water and dry bread. The children never ate so little at one meal in their lives before; and, to their surprise, their mother did not trouble herself about it; she only smiled, and said they would eat their dinner with a better appetite. Jane, however, secretly took a tea-spoonful of brown sugar, and spread it over Stephen's bread, that he, at least, might have something to give it a relish.

The table was set for dinner about twelve o'clock; when Ford, looking much the worse for his last night's debauch, and with a depression of spirits and sense of shame, that made him almost afraid to meet his children, presented himself below stairs. He threw himself into a chair, rested his head upon his hand, and said not a word to anybody. His wife was busied about her preparation for dinner, the children were all in the room, and presently little Stephen ran to his father and began to climb on his knee.

When dinner was ready, Ford, who still continued to sit where he was, said he could not eat anything.

" There is but very little for anybody," said his wife. " Come, draw in your chair."

Ford replied, very shortly, that he had no appetite.

His wife suspected he was out of humour—perhaps because she was a little out of humour herself; and she said, not without bitterness, " That he did quite right to sit where he was: he had very good reason to be ashamed of himself, seeing what a drunken fool he had been."

Oh, how easy it is to say the unkind word, and the word out of season! Mrs. Ford repented of it the moment she had spoken. A kind word, a look even of affection, sympathizing with him, and pardoning his weakness, would have melted him, like a child, into tears. His wife's words, and the look of severity that accompanied them, roused him into passion. He started up, throwing little Stephen from his knees, rather than setting him down, clenched his fists, and vowed that he would not be preached to by her nor by anybody else!

" And a pretty pass would you soon bring things to !" said his wife, "and let you go on in your own way."

Ford said she had better hold her tongue, for he could tell her at once, that he was in no humour to be provoked; that he would spend his money, for the future, how he liked and where he liked; nor would he be tied to any woman's apron-string, let her think herself as clever as she would !" His wife replied with bitterness, and one severe word led to another.

The children looked terrified, and their hearts beat violently; little Stephen set up a violent fit of crying, and Mrs. Ford, excited by the anger of her husband, whipped him, and then gave Jane a box on the ear because she interfered in his behalf; while Ford, up-braiding his wife with what he called the violence of her temper, snatched his hat from the table, and, banging the door after him, went out.

It was the most wretched meal that the Fords had ever sat down to.

Poor Mrs. Ford! It seemed to her as if, at the moment when she was trying to do the very best for her family, everything was beginning to go awry. She thought that she herself had done nothing wrong; for it is very difficult to persuade oneself that one is in error at any time, much more so when one is angry. It seemed to her no use striving, either to save money

or to get on in the world, for that her husband, some
way or other, would ruin all. She began to think
herself unhappy and unfortunate, and as if she must,
against her own best and most sincere desires, sit still
and let ruin, if it would, come down upon them.

Ford did not come home till all the children were
in bed; and when he came, she was sitting ruminating
as we have just mentioned, and crying between whiles.
Ford's shoes were very dirty, and he had a little
nosegay of spring flowers in his hand. He had not
then again been drinking: he had been to Clifton
Grove or Colwick Wood; he looked pale and unhappy.
How very soon is the spring of kindness and affection
reached in a woman's heart! Mrs. Ford never loved her
husband more than she did at that moment: he read
it in her eyes, though neither the one nor the other
spoke.

A piece of meat, part of the unfortunate dinner, had
been set aside for Ford: this his wife brought out and
set before him, together with a mug of ale.

"Now eat, John," said she, "for I am sure you
are tired and hungry; and, Heaven knows, I have been
very unhappy since you went. It will do me good to
see you eat—indeed it will! You know I love you,
John—I'm sure you do," said she laying her hand on
his shoulder.

"Why do you provoke me, then?" said he; "I am
sure you have no right to reproach me. I should like
to know where is the man who is a better father or
husband than I?"

"I am sure, John," said she, "I am heartily sorry
if I reproached you; but oh, you do not know how I felt,
just then, your being in liquor, and having lost your
money." She thought it was not then the moment
for her to unfold all her scheme of the bonnet-shop,
and her little plans of close economy; "but oh, I wish,
John," continued she, looking in his face with a countenance of sincere affection, "and this I say, not to
reproach you, but as I would say it to my own soul,

you would not let these men persuade you to go to the alehouse with a full pocket. You know, John, how good-natured you are—how easy it is to persuade you to drink on and on, after you have once passed a couple of glasses.   Look what a respectable man you are now; how happy we have lived, and how well we have brought up our children : don't you remember when the poor Jones'were just the same? and now—oh my God, John! when I think of this, it makes me almost beside myself."

" You are right, as you always are," said poor Ford, bursting into tears, " I have been a cursed fool; and when I think of Jones, I'm almost ready to join the Temperance folks."   His wife wept too; and she felt that, if the laying down of her life could benefit her husband, she would have gladly done it.

Ford wiped his eyes after a while, and said that his wife never said a truer word than when she called him a fool.

" Nay, John," replied she, " do not say so; and, as long as I live, I will never say such a word to you again."

" It was true," said he: " I was a fool to lose my money, when, Heaven knows how long I may have any to lose, if all's true that is said of the change that's coming over things."

" What! is it true then," said his wife, "that the lace-trade is getting bad?" for such a report had been current for months, although, as yet, the working-classes had experienced but small evidence of the fact.

" Yes," said her husband, "sure enough it is so. They read the papers at the Sir Isaac Newton; I went there to hear the speeches in Parliament read : there was a great deal said about these reports; the wisest among them fear a change; and, what is still worse, Martin and Wheeler have stopped!"

Had Mrs. Ford gone out into a neighbour's house this Sunday, or even gone into the street, she must have heard this news; for it rung through and through

Nottingham that day, like a knell; but as she had not, it came now to her ears like a terrible shock.

"Yes, sure enough it's all up with them," continued her husband; "not one of their hands have been paid this week. There were seven of them sent to the Sir Isaac, to ask what should be done. They had not one of them more money in their pockets than I—they had not a farthing to take home to their families!"

"It would be a dreadful thing," continued Ford, "if the lace-trade became bad; people were in very low spirits: they said there was but very little money stirring; and nobody was sure who would stand and who would not. Martin and Wheeler had bills out to the amount of 40,000*l*., and not one of them worth a penny. Their failure," he said, "would ruin many lesser houses. People were not sure at all about Weston's." Weston was the lace-manufacturer for whom Ford worked.

Mrs. Ford sate for some time in silence, quite astounded by what she had heard; she thought at length, it was by no means a bad time to unfold to her husband all her schemes. She put them in as attractive a light as she could; told him of Mrs. Dunnett, and the nice little shop, and how, last summer, she only turned and trimmed bonnets in her kitchen in Narrow Marsh, as she herself was now doing. She talked cheerfully of her own little shop, which she was determined next summer to have somewhere in some good part of the town; and how, for the next twelve months, she meant them all to work hard and save money; and thus, if any change did come, like prudent people, they should have made hay while the sun shone. She told him how she had resisted buying the tea-tray, and even shoes for little Stephen; and that she was determined not to buy any one thing for herself or for the children, which by any possibility they could do without. She said she had spoken to three or four people about recommending her, and she would mention it to the different shops in the neighbourhood, and

get John, who wrote such a neat hand, to write her a
few circulars, which she would send about; and that
she would put up a paper also at the entrance of the
court—Mrs. Higgins had done so; and how well she
had managed about letting her lodgings. Jane, she
said, should learn the business, and, as she was so
clever with her needle, she would soon be a good
assistant. Did not her husband think it a nice little
scheme? she asked; adding, that she could manage a
shop very well, she was sure—she knew very well what
was the principal requisites of a shop-keeper—what
had he now to say? But before he answered her, she
went on to tell him, that all this was in her mind, with
the very great desire she felt to make her family prosperous and respectable, when she was so vexed about
his having lost his money.

Ford was not quite so enthusiastic in his reply as his
wife wished. "Dunnett," said he, "had got money in
some lottery—he had heard it talked of last summer;
and he did not think, let his wife save as she would,
that she ever would save money enough for a shop: it
was quite out of the question, and he wondered how
ever she could think of such a thing.

The truth was, Ford was by no means an enthusiastic
man—he was a man without enterprise. To him his
wife's scheme seemed a great undertaking; the carrying of it out would be attended with a deal of trouble,
and would require sacrifices from every one of them;
and then, two to one, after all it might not succeed.
He was one to see immediately the difficulties and
disadvantages of a thing; he called himself prudent,
but the fact was, he was timid. His wife, on the contrary, always looked on the bright side of things; and
if, in the first instance, the difficulties of an undertaking
did not sufficiently present themselves to her, she had
courage to face them when they really came, and
stability to overcome them afterwards.

She was at once disappointed and mortified by the

coolness with which her husband received her communications.

"I tell you it never will do!" said he, as she continued to argue in favour of her plan, with what he thought pertinacity; "women are never satisfied to let well alone. I tell you, Dunnett had plenty of money to begin with; and I dont want the trouble and cumber of a shop."

"But suppose," said his wife, "the lace-trade really should get bad, and your wages should decrease, what would become of us?"

"You can get as much money as you please," said her husband, "and so can Jane—I am sure there is no harm in that; and John, if Weston will take more hands, can work also; he already understands something of a machine: but as to the shop, I don't like it at all, and that's the long and short of it!"

"I did not think you would have thrown cold water on it in this way, John," said his wife, struggling violently with herself to avoid being angry; "but I'm quite sure and certain, that if I were left to myself and had no need to ask anybody's consent or advice—I could manage it all nicely. I only wish I had thought of it five years ago, and could have got you in the mind, then we might have been rich people by this time!"

"Rich people!" repeated her husband, with a smile that was rather like a jeer.

"Yes," continued she, "I say rich people, if it had only come into our minds to save money then. Only think, John, what money you got in those days; and it's all gone, and one seems no better for it."

"That's just the way with women," said Ford. "Why, what in the world would you have? here you make a pretty riot if I only drink a glass or two of beer, and yet you have a house full of furniture, and plenty of good clothes, and you talk of having nothing to show! I wish you had a husband like Jones, or hundreds and thousands besides, and then you'd learn to be satisfied!"

Mrs. Ford feared that her husband was getting angry again; and, determining nevertheless not to drop the scheme of the bonnet-shop, thought it best for the present to say nothing more about it.

Jane, by her mother's orders, and greatly to her own satisfaction, began to learn the straw-bonnet business the very next week, and John went with his father to Weston's factory. Mr. Weston said he thought it a pity that Ford, seeing what a sober, industrious man he was, and what great wages he had earned so long, had not saved a little money to put his son apprentice to a good trade; for there were too many lace-hands already in the market, and if things went on as they seemed to be beginning, there would soon be no work for the fathers, say nothing of the sons.

Ford told his son, therefore, that it was no use his staying there—that he had better go to school for another quarter, and then they could see how things were by midsummer.

Before midsummer the trade of Nottingham received a severe check. Manufacturers began to find that they had over-supplied the market both at home and abroad. There was nowhere any demand for lace, and the frames in which it had been made either now stood idle or were sold in bankrupt's stock for one third of their first cost. The great failure of Martin and Wheeler involved, as was expected, many other houses in its ruin, and Westons, though they still stood, carried on their business on a much more cautious and contracted system. Every supernumerary hand was dismissed, and the wages of those who were retained were lowered to the utmost moderation. The "good times" were gone by, and everybody said that ruin was impending over the trade of the town; that, before long, no master would employ his men more than half their time, and that a dreadful winter—such a winter, in fact, as had never been known, might be expected.

In the decreased state of his wages, Ford himself proposed that his son should leave school and do something for his own maintenance; so he took him again with him to the factory, and set him to work in an old frame, as his apprentice.

One day Mrs. Ford went into Mrs. Dunnett's shop; she went as if to match some ribbon, but in fact to have a little talk with the mistress of the shop. The daughter sate as usual behind the counter, lining a bonnet, and Mrs. Dunnett was looking over a great number of bundles of straw-plat which she had been purchasing. Mrs. Ford matched her ribbon, and then began to say what a pretty shop it was, how well situated, and what fortunate people they were.

Mrs. Dunnett was much pleased to hear the shop praised, for it was a sort of family idol. She said yes, they were very fortunate people; it was a great mercy when people could feel their families thus provided for. It had been, she said, her husband's object for these twenty years.

"And the prize in the lottery," said Mrs. Ford, "must have been a great lift."

"Bless you!" exclaimed Mrs. Dunnett, "we never got a prize in the lottery—not we! Folks said so, because they did not like—they could not believe—it was all got by thrift and industry. My husband always saved money; he put in benefit societies and all kinds of societies, where he could save his money, and when the Savings Bank was established here, he put all his savings in that. He saved loads of money while the lace-trade was so brisk. God help those who did not," said she, "for sure enough the good times are over."

Mrs. Ford heaved a deep sigh, and Mrs. Dunnett, who did not notice it, went on. "No, we never got any prize in the lottery: my husband would not so have risked his money; he was always for saving; if he spent five shillings in a year in drink, that was the outside; I never saw him drunk in my life."

"Perhaps you had money left you?" said Mrs. Ford,

almost wishing to discover that the Dunnetts had not
done so much for themselves. ·

"Not a penny!" said Mrs. Dunnett. We've no
rich relations. I'll tell you you what my husband and
me had in our pockets on our wedding-day: shall I?"

"Do," replied Mrs. Ford.

"Three-halfpence!" said Mrs. Dunnett, laying great
emphasis on the words; " I had a penny and he had a
halfpenny. ' Never mind, my lass,' says my husband,
says he, singing the old song—

> ' We'll never ask help from man, woman, or parish!
> Yet we'll be worth something before that we die.'

We had good health, bless the Lord," continued Mrs.
Dunnett, " and so had our children, and we had seven,
five of them now living, and, please God, I hope will
all take good ways."

"Well, to be sure!" exclaimed Mrs. Ford, " I'm sure
it's as good as hearing a sermon."

Mrs. Dunnett liked to talk of these things; she was
beginning to be a little vain of their prudence, so she
continued. " Yes, as I said, we've all been a saving
family. I put my two daughters 'prentice to the bonnet-making business; Susan, there, was out of her time
last spring, and she began her trade last summer in
Narrow Marsh. We had the promise of this shop
then, as soon as it was at liberty, but we wanted to get
our hands in, as the saying is: Susan has saved already
a good bit of money. How much have you, Susan?"
asked she of her daughter.

" Four pounds, three and sixpence," replied Susan;
" three pounds in the Savings Bank, and three-and-
twenty shillings and sixpence in the Provident Society."

" I give her small wages as a journey-woman," said
Mrs. Dunnett; " she saves all that ever she can, and
her father says, when she has saved five-and-twenty
pounds she shall have a little share in the business.
It's a good thing, you know, to give one's children a motive for saving; young people are only too much given

to spend. I dare say you have found that out with your own. Bless me!" continued she, "and not young folks only but old ones also! Its quite shocking to think how little working-people ever think of saving!"

Mrs. Dunnett might have said a great deal more, had not a customer just then come in. Mrs. Ford went out, thinking with herself, " Well, I never heard anything in all my days equal to that!"

At night she told her husband what she had heard, and how the Dunnetts really had won no money in the lottery. He said it was very strange; but that Dunnett was a curmudgeon sort of person; he should not wonder if it was all true. He knew he never would drink with anybody; there was not a single workman who liked him. He wished, nevertheless, that they themselves had thought of saving before. Why did not the collectors for the Provident Society call at their house? He said he did not care if he himself began to save; he could take his money to the Savings Bank. Mr. Weston had often pursuaded him to do so; several of the men left some of their wages in his hands, for he had a deal to do with the Savings Bank, and he put it in for them. But now really, he said a man could get so very little, he did not know how he was to save.

" If it's only a shilling a week," said his wife, " do it. Once make a beginning, John, and we shall go on. I will tell the ladies of the Provident Society to call here, and I also will put something by weekly. Times without end have they looked in and asked me, but someway I did not like it; they used to be always preaching about economy and extravagance, and one of them said it was a pity we had laid out so much money in furniture; and another said it was a pity I had such a smart cap on, and that working people should dress their children plainly, and all that sort of thing. I was quite offended; but, dear me, I'm sure I see it all plain enough now, and I wish I had followed their advice; and so I might have done," added she willing to exculpate herself, " if they had not directly began to censure me. Mrs. Jones said it was just the same with her; they blamed her because the house was so badly furnished and the children so poorly dressed, never giving it a moment's thought that she had a bad husband. But the same ladies don't go round now, I see them every Monday in the court, and I'll begin next week—that I'm determined!"

It made Mrs. Ford quite happy that her husband entered into the saving scheme so cordially; she had feared he would not. The only drawback was, that unfortunately there was now so very little to save.

All summer long Mrs. Ford and her daughter worked hard at their business; but, what with Mrs. Dunnett's new shop, and what with about a dozen other new bonnet-makers who had sprung up in the neighbourhood of Bartram's Court, as if, said poor Mrs. Ford, in opposition to her, but principally in consequence of the trade of the town being in a very depressed state, the bonnet-making did not turn out as profitable as she had hoped. For some time she had been obliged to lay out the income of her little business in purchasing a small assortment of ribbons; the assortment was small, but at the end of the season the remainder on hand was greater than she had hoped for; that was so much dead stock till the next spring, when she must sell them at a reduced price, because all her customers knew them for the "fashions of the last year." If trade had been as good as usual, she would have needed twice as much; and, profiting now by experience, she purchased but very few winter ribbons. She had also on hand a little stock of straw-plat, and a number of blocks on which to shape bonnets, and perhaps thirty shillings worth of other materials.

Besides what might be considered her stock in trade, at the end of three quarters of a year, that is, by Christmas, she had, in the hands of the Provident Society, three pounds, eleven shillings—she never had felt so rich before. The baby, by this time, ran about alone. Jane was become a very expert assistant. The

o

secretary in the kitchen, with all its drawers, was full
of the articles of her trade; and she was now contemplating buying a sort of cupboard with a glass
front, to stand upon the dining-table, to hold, and to
display at the same time, her caps and bonnets.

Ford was sincere when he told his wife that he also
would begin to save. He told Mr. Weston the same;
and, most weeks, five shillings was reserved from his
wages for this purpose. He was astonished at the
consequence it gave him in his own eyes, when he
thought that he had money in the bank. He and his
wife sate by the fire at night, after the children were
gone to bed, and talked together of their earnings, and
of what they would do in the future. Alas! that poor
Ford and his wife begun their plans of economy and
prudence so late.

The winter came on—not more severe, certainly,
than winters usually are—but there was a gloom and
anxiety in people's minds, that made them think it so.
Fresh failures of manufacturers took place almost every
week. Shops were shut up, and houses became vacant
everywhere. Executions for rent were of daily occurrence, and pawnbrokers' shops were full of goods, which
people in their first distress had raised money upon.

As yet, however, the working-class were too new to
the want and misery, which from this time fell heavier
and heavier upon the town, to know exactly how it
was to be borne. They spent their diminished wages
still in eating and drinking, and, where they had not
money enough to pay, took goods on trust, pawning
their furniture and clothes to pay when the day of
reckoning came; whilst, as is always the case in times
of distress, beer-shops and gin-shops were opened on
all hands, and begun to reap a fertile harvest.

People said it would be a dreadful winter: they
wished it was spring; they thought that when spring
came things would begin to mend. Alas! they did not
know that this winter was only just the very beginning
of sorrows.

CHAPTER VI.

HOW THINGS WENT ON AT MRS. HIGGINS'S, AND A FIRST WRONG STEP.

THE last time we looked in at Mrs. Higgins's, Mrs. Greaseley had lodged there about six months, and was allowing poor Letty to turn over the treasures in her curious old-fashioned box.

Mrs. Greaseley was by no means passionately fond of children, though our readers may, perhaps, have imagined her so. If that had been the case, she would have made acquaintance with the Fords; it is true, she now and then gave Stephen bread and butter and sugar, but that did not induce the child to go often and visit her. He felt—for children feel those things instinctively—that Mrs. Greaseley endured his company rather than wished for it; so he volunteered her no visits. All the love that her heart contained for children, she said, was centred in the memory of her dead little boy, " her angel in heaven," as she called him; and she had no wish even to love a child, for his sake. Had Letty appeared before her full of health and strength, and with the usual attributes of childhood about her, Mrs. Greaseley very probably would have closed her heart against her, lest she should come like a rival to her soul's idol; but there was no danger with Letty: she was ten years old, deformed and lame, and with a sort of haggard melancholy face, that had not the remotest pretensions even to good looks. She seemed to be ill-used and disliked by every one, and came, therefore, to Mrs. Greaseley's knowledge as a creature with claims on her compassion—not her love. " Had she been a dog or a cat," said the good old lodger, " it would have been just the same—I must have taken her part, and have let her find a sort of asylum with me."

In the winter-time, when the weather was bad, Letty never went to school, and then she sate with Mrs.

Greaseley all day long. By degrees the good woman
became accustomed to the child's countenance, and
by degrees also came to think it less plain than at
first.

"I do believe," thought she to herself, "Letty
would be almost pretty if those people down stairs
did not worry and teaze her so, and drive her into
such dreadful passions; when she sits, and one only
looks at her face, one is quite surprised to see what a
pleasant countenance she has : I used to think her so
old and haggish looking!"

The truth was, that the influence of kindness had
excited amiable sentiments in her heart, and it was
the expression of these on the countenance which
improved it so much. Mrs. Greaseley was right; poor
Letty looked almost pretty, when, with her heart full
of affection, she sate at her work in the room of the
kind old lodger.

The good old woman would sit at her work, and
tell Letty all about her youth; how she had lived in
London in service, and of all the wonders of London;
of St. Paul's and the Tower, of play-houses and
parks, till Letty's brain was all in a whirl of delicious
wonder, and till her usually sallow and hollow cheeks
glowed, and her large dark eyes, usually so dull and
dead, were lit up with intelligence. It was no wonder
that Mrs. Greaseley thought her so much improved.
It amused her also, to have such a visitor, for she
would have had nobody to talk to if it had not been
for Letty; and now she never had talked so much in
all her life before. It was a great pleasure for her to
talk of past times; and, only to know that her narratives
and her reminiscences found a ready listener, made her
at all times ready to begin.

By degrees she conceived the idea of trying to
recover Letty of her lameness; alas! to amend her of
her deformity was out of the question. Among her
husband's books Mrs. Greaseley knew there was one
on medicine and surgery. She examined the poor

girl's lame hip, and even talked with her mother about its cause; and came at last to the opinion that it originated in weakness, and had become chronic by neglect. She knew that she lived better, that she allowed herself better food than Mrs. Higgins's parsimony provided for her family; she determined, therefore, that now and then, when her husband was out, Letty should eat with her, and that every day she would sponge her lame hip with cold water, in which she would dissolve a handful of salt.

She exacted a promise from Letty to tell this to nobody; she could not exactly explain to herself why she wished Mrs. Higgins and Mima not to know of it: most likely it was, that as neither of them were favourites with her, she did not wish to seem to do them a kindness, even in the person of Letty; or she might fear, that they too would be expecting something or other from her, because so many people, as the proverb says, "if you give them an inch, look for an ell also." She knew very well, however, why she did not wish her husband to know; he was, as she had told Letty, a very exact man; he was one who, as he often said himself, had no notion of doing anything for nothing. It would have made him angry to think that Letty Higgins ate of his bread and drank of his cup. He allowed his wife no more money than he thought just enough for her own necessities; and would have deducted a something from her allowance if he had thought she could afford to give anything away. He had, beside this, taken a dislike to poor Letty: it would not have displeased him to have seen Mima up stairs, because he always said she was such a pretty girl; and he sometimes even chucked her under the chin; so, when he was at home, Letty never went up stairs.

Mrs. Higgins, very well satisfied that Letty should be a favourite with the old woman, and with sagacity enough very soon to discover the husband's peculiar character, seconded all this understood, but secret arrangement, without saying a word to any one, or attempting at all to pry into her lodger's motives; thus, in every respect Letty's situation was improved.

We have told how Mrs. Greaseley permitted Letty, for the first time, to look into one of her locked-up boxes; the effect of that permission did not soon wear away; nay, it almost influenced the whole of her life, as the progress of her story will show.

There was nothing of any great value in the box into which Letty had looked, but for weeks and months its contents were of unsatiating interest; she soon learned to open the secret spring herself, and fathom the mysteries of the first little drawer; the second she was not again permitted to open. Mrs. Greaseley said "she had done wrong already to open it; her husband would be so angry if he knew, and that she would not dare to tell him for ever so much!"

Letty never examined the contents of this box without longing to peep into her mother's desk. She thought of it almost night and day; she often used to dream that she had got her mother's keys and had opened it; sometimes she dreamed that it was full of the most unimaginable and beautiful things; sometimes she dreamed only of horrors—of having a difficulty in getting the key into the lock—of being plagued with all sorts of impediments and pains; and then, when at last the desk was opened, that it contained only spiders and little vipers, that came curling out from every drawer to bite her, and centipedes, that ran nimbly out and covered her hands and arms in a minute. Again and again these dreams came—sometimes for several nights in succession, and sometimes only now and then; but always, through the whole of the next day, whether the dream had been pleasant or horrible, her mind was haunted, as it were, with a feverish desire to know really what this wonderful desk contained. Some way or other, she dared not tell all this to Mrs. Greaseley; she thought that if she knew she would be angry, and fear was almost as strong a passion with the poor girl as curiosity. She therefore kept this in her own heart, and made the compact with herself, that whenever she could get her mother's keys, she would know really, in broad, good daylight, what every drawer and box in their rooms contained, and then she thought she should be satisfied.

She had not been for twelve months in habits of such familiar intercourse with Mrs. Greaseley, without having seen to the bottom of every drawer and box in her room. She knew all that they contained, had seen every gown that Mrs. Greaseley had, and had heard, over and over again, where they were bought, and on what extraordinary occasions they had been first worn.

Letty used to amuse the old woman by telling her, when the chest of drawers was locked, what it contained; here this and that piece of clothing lay, what lay above it, and what below, till she would laugh, and say Letty had such a wonderful headpiece! she thought she knew more about the things than she did. There was now not a single mystery left to Letty in these two rooms, excepting the little leathern bag in that second little drawer, in the old walnut-tree box; how she came to penetrate even that, we must now relate.

Mrs. Greaseley, as we said before, very rarely went out, excepting on Saturdays and Sundays, and then Mrs. Higgins was at home. It happened, however, on one certain Monday afternoon, she wanted some worsted to finish the stockings she was knitting; Mima was at school, and Mrs. Higgins was out washing, and Letty, though she was better of her lameness, could not go so far as the market-place, at least not alone. Letty said, cheerfully, that she would stop in the house; that she would lock the door inside, and not once go out; nor would she speak to any one

through the window: she said she was not at all afraid;
nay, even that she should like to stay. She was, in
reality, very anxious to be left alone, for Mrs. Greaseley's
keys happened—a very unusual circumstance—to be
left hanging in the corner cupboard door, and the idea
at once flashed into her mind, that with these she
could, perhaps, open her mother's desk. One present
anxiety, however, she had, and that was, lest Mrs.
Greaseley should see them and take them out before
she went; she set about as if to make the room
quite orderly, and hung an apron, which had been
flung over a chair-back, upon the keys, as if on a hook.
The good old woman put on her bonnet and cloak in
the next room, and then, throwing a shovel-full of ashes
on the fire, and telling Letty to be sure not to meddle
with it while she was away, went out, never noticing
the apron, nor missing the keys.

Letty turned the house-door key in its lock after
she was gone, and also, to make all doubly sure, bolted
the door; and then, with a heart beating almost
audibly, took the keys from the cupboard-door, and
came down stairs again. Her hand trembled so, she
could hardly direct a key into the lock of the desk;
at 'last she forcibly steadied it, but there was no
key that fitted; one after another she tried, but in
vain; one was too large, another was too small. It
was the same with the drawers under the desk—was
the same with the chest in the lean-to; there was no
one key that would fit any one of her mother's locks.
When should she have such an opportunity again?
She tried every key again, but to no purpose. What
should she do? She had hoped to have had all these
long-haunting mysteries unravelled—she found them
sealed as if even with seven seals. She was consumed, as it were, by a desire after forbidden knowledge. Mrs. Greaseley had told her the history of
Blue-beard and his seven wives; she never thought
of it, however, then, or she might have been frightened;

and while she stood there in a fever of vexation and disappointment, suddenly the idea flashed into her mind, that if she could not see her mother's secret possessions, she could certainly look into the forbidden drawer up stairs—could even look into Mr. Grease-ley's leathern bag.

She was in no humour to give ear to her conscience, let it ask her what questions it might; so, hurrying up stairs, she hastily glanced out at the window, to see that nobody was coming, and then, possessing herself of the secret key, with a hand that shook like an aspen leaf, unlocked and opened the drawer. All was as it had been nearly twelve months before: there lay the watch, looking just as when she held it that day so long in her hand; she dared not take it up now, however, lest she should drop it; and there lay the leathern bag, drawn up tightly, with the strings wound round it. It felt heavy—there must be a deal of money in it, she thought. But, oh! if anybody came! She ran to the window to look out—nobody was coming; she listened—all was profoundly still; she opened the bag—what a deal of money there seemed to be in it—gold, and silver, and even copper! she put in her hand and lifted up a handful, and still there was a deal more!

It was all a hurried, fearful pleasure. She could not tell, she was sure, how time had gone; it might be hours since Mrs. Greaseley went, or it might only be minutes. She grew terrified, and, drawing together the strings of the bag, wound them round it again. She thought to put it back, when the idea occurred to her—suppose Mr. Greaseley had some secret way of laying it there—had some secret way of fastening the strings—and she should thus be found out! She wished she had only noticed exactly how it was done; she tried to remember, but she was too much agitated to recall anything.

Mrs. Greaseley will be here in a moment! thought she, what shall I do? She put the bag in, locked the drawer, fastened the spring, locked the box, set it again in its accustomed place, replaced the little key, relocked that drawer, and put the key in the cupboard-door, not forgetting to throw the apron again on the chair-back, lest, on her return, Mrs. Greaseley should notice the singular circumstance of its hanging on the keys. All this was done in the utmost haste and agitation; she felt ready to drop, and, chancing to see her face in the looking-glass, saw that she looked deadly pale; she rubbed her cheeks, therefore, till they burnt with an unnatural redness, and then she was more frightened than ever.

She had just sense enough left, to know that the best way was to be calm; Mrs. Greaseley was not yet come; perhaps she would not come for some minutes; she would stand against the window, therefore, and try not to think of what she had been doing; and after all, if she could only get calm, and not tremble so much, nor look so guilty, how could Mrs. Greaseley know anything about it?

She stood at the window and looked out. Harriet Jones was fetching water from the pump in a broken jug; she was nodding at somebody, and looking very merry; Stephen Ford was hopping about with a broken pea-stick. "Oh dear!" exclaimed she to herself, "that I was as easy in my mind as they!"

Presently Mrs. Greaseley turned into the court and came directly across to the door. Letty felt as if a shot had passed through her at the sight; but she went down stairs nevertheless, and with a trembling hand unlocked the door; and, forgetting that she had bolted it also, tried to open it.

"Why did you bolt the door?" asked Mrs. Greaseley, when at length it was unfastened.

"I don't know," said Letty, looking greatly disconcerted, "but I was so frightened."

"Nothing was likely to come to you," said Mrs. Greaseley, again locking the door, as was customary.

Letty said she wanted to wash her hands, and went

into the lean-to, while Mrs. Greaseley went up stairs. She did not wash her hands, however, but sate down on the chest; she thought she was not half calm enough to face her friend; she felt as if the truth were sure to come out; and, "Whatever will become of me!" exclaimed she internally, ready to burst into tears.

Presently she heard Mrs. Greaseley's voice at the top of the stairs, calling her; she was terrified out of her senses; she thought, somoway or other, she was found out, and, then, without answering, went up stairs, hardly conscious of what she was doing. Mrs. Greaseley had the hanks of worsted in her hand, and said she wanted Letty to hold them. "But dear me! what's amiss with you?" exclaimed she, seeing how strange was the expression of her countenance.

"Nothing is amiss with me!" returned the girl, "nothing at all!"

Mrs. Greaseley thought she had perhaps been frightened with being left alone; she said nothing, however, and gave her the worsted to hold. It was not finished when Mrs. Greaseley began to think of her tea; she said she would go and get it; and Letty, wishing to make herself useful, to make amends in every way that she possibly could, for her breach of trust, said she would put the worsted over two chairs and finish winding it.

Mrs. Greaseley went to the corner cupboard for the tea-things, and while she had yet her hand in her pocket, feeling for the keys, perceived them already in the door. She was greatly surprised, for she was not in the habit of leaving them anywhere, but still more was she surprised when she found a wrong key in the lock.

"How's this?" said she, after she had tried to turn the key in vain. Letty knew instantly, that in her terror she had made the mistake. "How's this?" said she, turning to her, "have you been to the cupboard?"

" No," said Letty, quickly, but not in her natural
tone.

" Haven't you had the keys?" asked Mrs. Greaseley.

" I've never touched them," said Letty, terrified
into telling a direct falsehood.

Mrs. Greaseley knew instantly that she did not speak
the truth, but supposed she had been looking at an
earthenware shepherd and shepherdess that she greatly
admired. The good woman had the utmost forbearance and charity; she thought it was no great crime if
she had done so; she knew how severe Letty's mother
was with her, and that she would not have dared to
confess such a thing to her, for fear of punishment; so,
pitying the unhappy child's weakness, she said no more;
whilst Letty, who knew that she had done too much—
almost too much to be forgiven, if all was known, tried
all in her power, by a hundred little assiduities, to make
amends for her crime.

That night, as Letty lay in her bed, she tossed about,
and could not sleep; for the idea came into her mind
all at once, like a flash of lightning—suppose after all she
had not locked the little money-drawer! She could
not remember turning the key; she knew that she
shut it and took the key out, but she could not help
fearing, that in her trepidation she might have forgotten to lock it, and then she should be found out, and
found out by Mr. Greaseley too! and what would he
say, not to her only, but to his wife also? She had
put the wrong key in the cupboard door—that was a
proof how very little she knew what she was doing.
The more she thought, the more probable appeared
this terrific chance: " What would become of her!
what should she do!" said she to herself, in an agony of
mind that drove away all power of sleep.

Her mother was angry, and so was Mima; and the
former declared that Letty should sleep up stairs in the
garret, as sure as she was born; for that, to get a wink
of sleep with her in the bed was quite impossible,

Letty tried to be still; the hot tears, which she dared not wipe away, rolled to the bolster till it was quite wet; and only, at length, an hour or two after midnight, when she was cramped with lying long in an uneasy position, could she get to sleep, and then to dream of Mr. Greaseley, in the form of a great dog, falling upon her and tearing her to pieces, and then to wake in terror that made her fear to sleep again.

Very anxious indeed were the days that succeeded; but Mr. Greaseley came and went, and not a word was said, while Mrs. Greaseley was as kind as ever. By degrees, therefore, Letty herself began to tranquillize, even though her mother, true to her threat of making her sleep in the garret by herself, within the next week bought a stump-bedstead, and set it in that upper room, declaring that the first sale there should be in the neighbourhood, she would buy a mattrass and blankets, and then Letty should go there and disturb nobody.

CHAPTER VII.

THE FRAME AT HOME.

As time went on, the amendment in Letty's lameness and in her general appearance were astonishing; she could walk a considerable distance with only a stick; and, in process of time, Mrs. Greaseley began to hope, would be comparatively strong and independent of help. The neighbours all remarked the change; everybody, someway or other, had come to know that Mrs. Greaseley had been the cause of it, and all said Mrs. Higgins could never do enough for her lodger. Mrs. Higgins did feel obliged, certainly; but the sense of gratitude was by no means oppressive; had she done only half as much for Mima, the case would have been different.

Mima Higgins had, by this time, thrown off all appearance of the girl; she believed herself a handsome

H

young woman—lady she would have called herself. She worked at lace-mending, at a lace warehouse, with between twenty and thirty other girls; getting thus her own living, and being, as she said, entitled to dress and do just as she pleased.

With all Letty's improvement, she never would be other than a poor dwarfish and hump-backed thing— so said Mima, and so said Mrs. Higgins, " but for all that," said her mother, " she must do something for her own maintenance—there was no doubt about that!"

Mrs. Higgins and her two daughters were sitting by their fire, one wet Sunday afternoon, and Mima had a smart muslin collar in her hand, which she had purchased the day before, and at which she had now been looking.

" I wish I had such a one!" said Letty.

" Lord! what should you do with such a one!" exclaimed her sister, and smiled, as Letty thought, in derision. The poor girl was beginning to be sensitive on the score of personal appearance; she tried to lower her shoulders, and sit upright, and then coloured almost crimson, because the attempt was so ineffectual.

" Yes, Letty," said her mother, taking no notice of her discomposed looks, " when you can get your own bread, as Mima does, then you may buy your own clothes; but I see no reason," added she, " why, even now, you should not do something; you have got quite strong now—you must work!"

" That I will gladly do," returned Letty. " I am so much better now, I can walk as far as the warehouse; I will go there every day with Mima; I shall be so glad to have money of my own, and buy things for myself!"

Mima said, if Letty went with her to the warehouse, she must go in her Sunday things, for that all the girls dressed handsome; Mr. Warrington himself, she said, never liked to see people shabby about the place; and after all, added she, the next moment, it was ten to one if Letty got employment there, for they would laugh at her—all the girls at Mr. Warrington's were so pretty.

Again Letty coloured deeply, and felt oppressed by a painful consciousness; she wished she knew how to make herself look like other people; but she said not a word of her feelings, either to her mother or sister, but talked cheerfully to them of going to work on the morrow, and tried to make the thought agreeable to herself, in the very novel circumstance of beginning by this means to earn a little money.

Mrs. Greaseley was not told of the new arrangement that night, because her husband was at home, but the next morning Letty went up to announce it, and to say good-bye at the same time. Mrs. Greaseley said she was very sorry—she wished they had mentioned it to her; it would have been far better for her to have had a frame at home: the truth was, the kind old woman was sorry to part with her home-companion.

The house seemed very solitary after she was gone, and Mrs. Greaseley, for the first time, began to suspect that she had a strong affection for the girl.

Mr. Warrington, as Mima had said, shrugged his shoulders, and demurred as to whether Letty could have work; he said he would inquire, however, and in the . meantime she could go into the mending-room, and sit down. All the girls were at work when the two entered, for Mima had walked slowly, to accommodate her sister. Letty thought, indeed Mima had said true, when she said that all the girls at Mr. Warrington's were pretty. There was a general raising of heads as they entered; a general look of surprise, a whispering of one to another, and, as Letty thought, a general giggle. Mima told her to sit down upon a chair, which she pointed out to her, and then going to another part of the room, took off her bonnet and shawl, and arranged her long black ringlets by a looking-glass, which hung on the wall, and, sitting down on a vacant chair in a circle of five other girls, nodded and smiled, and said something to

her companions, who all seemed glad to see her, and
then began to help them in mending holes or defective
places in a large piece of unbleached net, which lay on
the ground among them.

The room was a very large one; and never had poor
Letty, in the whole course of her life, felt in so painfully awkward a situation. She had never been accustomed to be among strangers; she was bashful as a
child, and the consciousness of her own dwarfish stature
and remarkable deformity, became evident to all her
senses, as if the finger of every one of those seven-and-
twenty girls had been pointed at her in open derision.
A mind much stronger than poor Letty's might have
been unnerved by it; for it seemed to her that she sate
in the most conspicuous place in the whole room, whilst
the single circumstance of the chair being too high
for her to sit at ease upon, greatly increased her discomfort.

The girls kept working on; but every now and then
she was aware of an eye being cast upon her; of a
merry half-suppressed laugh, which, in the exaggerated
state of her feeling, she expected would spread round
the whole room. Why did Mima leave her there? thought
she to herself; why had she seated herself such a long
way off? Letty did not dare to speak to her; the bare
idea of speaking aloud was terrific. " If I should die
here," thought poor Letty, ready to burst into tears,
" I durst not speak." She felt almost delirious; there
seemed such a silence in the room; and yet, she knew
that everybody was thinking about her; and at the
same time the chair seemed as if it were growing
higher, and her legs becoming shorter! she felt that,
however ridiculous she might make herself, she certainly should cry before long!

The youngest girl in the room at that moment
looked round at her; it was Rachel Ford, who had
now worked there about a month. She had seen
Mima come in with her sister, and she had even smiled
with her companion; she knew she was sitting there;

every now and then she had glanced at her since; but, now she saw the poor creature's face of embarrassment and distress, she spoke out aloud.

" For shame! Mima Higgins," said she, addressing her across the room, "to let your poor sister sit there, a laughing-stock to everybody! But everybody knows that you are a conceited, set-up, unnatural thing—that you are!"

" She need not sit there," returned Mima; " but take her under your wing, and welcome, Miss Rachel!" said she, looking angry, and yet laughing.

" I don't want to take her under my wing!" said Rachel, who liked none of the Higginses, and was as sensitively alive to good looks as Mima herself, and who instantly thought, that perhaps if she established herself as Letty's champion, she would be wanting to walk home with her every day. " No, Mima Higgins!" said she, " I want to have nothing to do with any of your name, whether they are crooked or straight; but I hate to see a bad heart—that I do!" and then she began a whispered detail to her young companions, of all she heard, and all she ever had known against the Higginses.

Letty was more uncomfortable than ever, and was wiping away large tears with the back of her hand, because she was too nervous to get out her pocket-handkerchief, when Mr. Warrington came in, and, going up to Mima, said that they should not be able to find employment for her sister. The truth was, as Mima had said, Mr. Warrington liked to have pretty, healthy-looking girls in his rooms; his factory was a large one; foreigners who visited the town came to his place; he was a Nottingham man, born and bred, and was jealous of the honour and reputation of the town. He liked to impress everybody with the idea that it was the happiest place under the sun; he therefore would say to his visitors, " You see no cripples here—no pale, ill-fed, diseased creatures, as in

H 2

Manchester, Leeds, and those other towns; look to
the statistics of Nottingham, or rather look into my
factory, and you may judge for yourselves!" It had
been folly to think of his giving employment to poor
Letty; he would not have had her about the place, he
said to himself, if she would have worked for nothing.

"You must go home, Letty, there's no work for
you!" said Mima, going up to the chair where she sate.

Letty instantly wondered how should she ever get
out of the room; that would be quite as painful as
sitting to be stared at; she wished Mima would go out
with her, but she did not like to ask.

"Why don't you go?" said Mima, seeing her fold
her arms in her shawl, but make no step forward.

"I don't know the way out," said the poor girl, not
liking to confess the truth, which she feared would seem
ridiculous.

"It's easy enough to find the way out," said Mima;
"just the way you came in."

Letty mustered what seemed to her courage enough
for martyrdom; and, while her sister reseated herself to
her work, walked down that long room, and passed
those groups of girls, all of whom, not meaning it un-
kindly, suspended their work for a moment, to see her
go out. When she was fairly in the street, it seemed
to her that she would rather eat dry bread, and be
clothed in rags all the days of her life, than go again
into a mending-room.

On her return home she went straight up stairs, and
told Mrs. Greaseley all her disappointment and morti-
fication.

"I know," said she, "that I am a poor little object; I
feel it every day of my life; and I don't care if I never
go out again as long as I live! I almost wish I was
dead and buried!" said she, giving way to the bitterness of her feelings.

"You must not say so! You must not be wicked!"

said Mrs. Greaseley; " you did not make yourself, Letty, and therefore you must be patient. God made you, child, just as well as the angels in heaven; nor does he care for you one bit the less, because you are not so handsome as they are! You must wait his time, Letty; you must not be wicked, and wish for death—death comes soon enough, and often before he is wanted," said she, wiping her eyes—for she was thinking of her little son. " No, Letty, you must not grow wicked, else I shall not love you!"

" And if you do not love me," said the poor girl, bursting into tears, " who will?"

" You must go with me to church," said the good woman; who, believing this was the duty of every pious Christian, and often finding comfort in so doing herself, thought this was the true way to make Letty happy, and to teach her to bear her afflictions with patience. " My master," continued she, (for so she often called her husband,) " never goes to church; it would be much better for him if he did; he is at the Van Office on Sunday mornings—you can go with me ; I have two prayer-books, and, as I sit on the bench in the aisle, there is plenty of room for us both. It will do you good, child, to hear the word of God preached, and kneel down and say your prayers among Christian people."

Poor Letty continued to weep; nay, she wept more than ever, for she was touched by Mrs. Greaseley's kindness to her; and she remembered with shame and remorse, that she had, not only once, but now, alas! twice, looked clandestinely into that little money-drawer; and, the last time, had even counted out all the money, on to her knee! " I wish I had not done so! why did I? why was it any temptation to me? so as I suffered in my mind for weeks and weeks after-wards! oh, why did I do it?" Such were Letty's internal ejaculations. She felt unworthy of love—un-worthy of kindness, even—and she wept almost pas-

sionately. Mrs. Greaseley asked her why she cried
so; she had half a mind to fall down on her knees and
confess all, but she did not. She thought that she
would repent of it at church; that she would pray God
to forgive her, instead of asking forgiveness from Mrs.
Greaseley, who thus need know nothing about it.

Poor Letty! she said she did not know why she
was crying, but she thought it was because Mima was
so unkind.

This scheme of the lace-mending having failed,
Mrs. Higgins said they must think of something else,
for it was high time Letty worked for herself, She
was the more resolved upon this, because she had lost
one of her best places in the failure of Martin and
Wheeler, she having washed for five years at the
Martins', and brought home, as was her custom, a
piece of soap, and good store of cold victuals from
the house each time, to say nothing of the ample allowance of gin, which she also received. Mrs. Higgins,
who did not cook much herself, but was generally
supplied by what she brought home with her, began
now to find that everybody seemed to be getting
more economical : there was not half nor a quarter the
money stirring that there used to be : she found her
perquisites and emoluments decreasing every week;
servants, in all families, were better looked after; they
declared that there really was no cold meat to give
away now, for that the family themselves eat up every
scrap. Mistresses also began to come and go in and
out of the wash-houses themselves, to count the squares
of soap, and to mix the starch. The good times of
carelessness and plenty were gone by; people began
to look heedfully after their substance, now that it was
felt to be decreasing, and servants and washerwomen
made loud outcries.

" Lord !" exclaimed Mrs. Higgins, to all her acquaintance, " how things have changed within these few
years! I can't get my two shillings, much more my

half-crown for a day's washing, as I used to do! It's all over with washerwomen now-a-days."

Such being the state of things, it was doubly necessary that Letty should do something to maintain herself; but. after her experience in the mending-room, she declared she would not again go out to work, even if they would pay her in gold, but would have a frame at home, she said, as Mrs. Greaseley had mentioned. Her mother made no objection; nay, she was very well pleased; for, at home, any old clothes would do to wear, while if she went out, she would be wanting to dress as others did; and only look at Mima, how she dressed! Even her mother had exclaimed, the very last Sunday, when she saw the new silk gown come home, and saw her go out in it, in a new shawl and silk stockings; and when she said that the bonnet, which one of the bonnet-makers, whom Mrs. Ford called "opposition," had just turned and trimmed, was not good enough, and that she must have a new one from Mrs. Dunnet's! Mima was shamefully extravagant, said Mrs. Higgins, and so were the Fords, every one of them; but there was no reason why Letty should be so. She thought, therefore, that if Letty worked at home, one way or another, most, if not all of her incomings, would go directly into her pocket.

Mrs. Greaseley came down stairs one night. and proposed that. she and Letty should have a frame between them; she said she had often thought of working again at the trade; she understood it very well, and would instruct Letty; and next week they would have a quilling-frame, and thus she could get her hand in; and by the time it was finished, they would take some sprigging, and then have a veil-piece, which was the sort of work she liked best; she was quite sure she and Letty should get on nicely together.

It was all settled accordingly; a frame was engaged from a warehouse, with its piece of unbleached silk net rolled upon it. It was placed in its two tressels, by the window, in Mrs. Greaseley's room; and their two chairs stood side by side, opposite the light, and, with blunted needles, they began their work—the most elementary of all lace-work—that of whipping, or running threads of silk at equal distances, the whole length of the piece, by which, when it had been bleached and stiffened, it was divided into breadths or quilling.

Letty liked the work; she and her old friend worked cheerfully at it all the week, and, every Sunday morning, duly went to church together. The old woman repeated, with religious strictness, every response, and read every lesson; she told Letty she must do the same, and not look about her—not think of the people who were there. Letty meant to be very religious; she meant to pray for forgiveness for what she considered her great sin; she thought of it every time she went to church, but, someway or other, could not help looking at the tall church-aisle, and the pillars and the lofty windows; and listening to the organ, and glancing at the people, often made her forget to finish the prayer which, with a sincere desire to do right, she had begun. Letty thought that she must be a very wicked girl, because she found it so difficult to pray; and, especially, because Mrs. Greaseley used to say that a good person could no more help praying and giving thanks, than he could help breathing; she said that prayers were always good in people's hearts. At first Letty was very uncomfortable about this; she could not remember, that, however miserable having opened the money-drawer had made her, that she ever had repented of it before God, as Mrs. Greaseley said she always must, if ever she did wrong; still, she felt a tranquillity of mind—a consciousness of strength to resist temptation, which she had never felt before. I have never repented of my sin, said she, as I know I ought to have done, nor have I prayed God to forgive me, but I am sure I never shall do so again.

Although Letty was, as she said, "certain sure" that she never would open Mrs. Greaseley's money-drawer again, she was not quite as certain that she could resist the temptation to look into her mother's desk, if the opportunity offered, especially as she could not ascertain in her own mind whether that would be wicked or not. She knew how angry her mother would be if she did: whatever her reasons might be for so doing, she had kept its contents, she believed, a profound mystery from every one; her valuables were there, no doubt; her money was also there; and there, also, was Letty's money. The poor girl had felt it as a piece of almost cruel injustice when her mother had possessed herself of the money due to her for two different frames of work, and locked it up in her desk; she had fancied that, like Mima, she was to earn and spend, or keep at least, her own money; such did not appear to be her mother's intention: she remonstrated, but to remonstrate was vain; she cried, but her tears were to no purpose; she told Mrs. Greaseley, and the good woman sympathized with her, and that was at least some comfort.

They had now worked for some months on a veil-piece which, when completed, would bring them in about fifteen shillings each, and poor Letty thought how very rich she should be if she could only be allowed to keep this money. She was disappointed, however.

The weather was damp and cold, and Mrs. Greaseley dared not venture out, on account of her asthma; Mrs. Higgins said, therefore, she would call at the warehouse and receive the money for them. She received two half sovereigns and two five shilling pieces, and one of each she gave to Mrs. Greaseley; Letty held out her hand for hers: how beautiful that gold and silver coin looked! she could hardly prevent herself snatching it from her mother's hand.

" You will give Letty her money," said Mrs. Greaseley.

" I shall keep it for her," replied Mrs. Higgins.

" But it would encourage her to work," remonstrated the other, " if only now and then she could look at her money, say nothing about spending. You would take good care of your money, would you not, Letty?"

"I would not spend a sixpence," said Letty; "I would put it in a little tin box that I have, and keep it under my mattrass up stairs."

"I shall lock it up in my desk," said Mrs. Higgins.

"Let me keep it for her," said Mrs. Greaseley: "I know Letty sometimes would like to look at it and count it over; and I will take care she never spends any without asking your leave; will you Letty?"

"Not a sixpence—not a penny!" said Letty.

"I shall take care of it," returned Mrs. Higgins, and went down stairs. Letty followed her mother to the top of the stairs, and then, stooping down, looked into the kitchen and saw her take out the key, unlock the desk, which now seemed to her like a hateful dragon, ready to devour everything; and, after some little delay, just enough to open some of these mysterious little drawers and make the deposit safely, she saw the lid closed, and the keys again dropped into the large pocket by her mother's side.

"Ah!" exclaimed poor Letty, to herself, "if ever I do get those keys into my hands, I will rummage that desk, that I will, as sure as I am born!"

CHAPTER VIII.

MONEY SAVED, AND MONEY LOST.

WE are now arrived at the commencement of that winter, when all the family of the Fords were working so hard to save money. Letty and Mrs. Greaseley had now worked together above a year. Now and then Mrs. Higgins used to allow Letty part of her earnings but only now and then; she said Letty was too young and too inexperienced to have money; that she did not want it; she only went out now and then, besides going to church on a Sunday morning; and that, if she

was neat and clean, it was all that was necessary.
Letty thought it very hard, and so did Mrs. Greaseley,
that she might not at least count over her money; but
it was no use asking; Mrs. Higgins said " they might
keep their breath to cool their pottage, for that she
should keep the money,. and then she knew it was
safe."

One day Jane Ford came in to bring a bonnet which
had been turned, and stood to talk a little with them.

" You must be getting a deal of money now," said
she, " so hard as you work. What do you do with
your's, Letty?"

Letty said her mother kept it for her; she wished
she might keep it herself; she thought it very hard
that she might not.

" Why don't you give it to the ladies who come
about for the Provident Society?" asked Jane Ford.

" They don't come here now," said Letty; " they
teazed mother a long time, but she would not give them
a penny, and yet she has a deal of money, I do believe,
locked up in her desk."

" Mother always gives them money now," said Jane
Ford; " we did not use to, but we do now, and Rachel
and John, and all; and when it gets a good deal, we
shall put it into the Savings Bank, and then it will pay
interest, you know."

Letty did not know what interest was, but from what
Jane said, she knew that she meant there was some
advantage in it: and she said she wished her mother
would let her do so.

" It's your own money," said Jane, " and so as you
work all day long! I'm sure, if I were you, I would give
it to the Provident Society, unbeknown to my mother!"

Mrs. Greaseley said Mrs. Higgins would be very
angry if she knew what Jane had said to her daughter;
" but," said she, " I wish you would tell the Provident
ladies to call here; I don't mind if I myself put by
something."

Jane Ford said she would, and went out.

"Why does not Mr. Greaseley put his money in the Savings Bank?—he has such a deal!" asked Letty, hardly remembering what she was saying, but rather thinking aloud.

"What money?" asked Mrs. Greaseley, quickly.

Letty started, for she feared instantly that she had betrayed herself, and, with a guilty, frightened face, said, "his money in the little drawer there; didn't she remember showing it her years ago?"

Not showing you the money," said the old lodger, looking up from her frame with a face almost as agitated as Letty's, and taking off her spectacles, "the money I never showed you!"

"No, not the money!" said Letty, stammering, "the leather bag; I only meant the little leather bag!"

"You did not look into the bag, Letty?" asked the other.

"No," replied Letty, feeling almost sick, "I only meant the outside of the bag; you know I saw the outside of the bag."

"He would never forgive me," said Mrs. Greaseley, "if I let you, or anybody, look into his money-drawer; I never look into it myself; I don't know how much money he has, whether it is much, or whether it is little —that's no business of mine; and you cannot know either, child, how should you?"

Letty said she did not know anything about it, but she always fancied Mr. Greaseley rich; and that it was years since she had seen the bag; she said this, but she could not recover her composure all day, fearing that, some time or other, she might betray herself, and then she should lose Mrs. Greaseley's love for ever. She fancied that the old woman was less friendly all that day than common; but she was quite mistaken; Mrs. Greaseley believed every word she said, and was only calculating with herself, how much money in the course of the year she should save, if she put by so much a week; and, as she was no great arithmetician, it took her a long time to make the calculation.

The next day Letty had quite 'got over her fright, and began to revolve in her mind the idea of putting by something weekly in the Provident Society likewise. She mentioned it to her friend, and they both agreed that there could be no harm in proposing it to her mother.

To their great surprise, Mrs. Higgins said she had no great objection; she thought indeed, that it would be a good thing; Letty should put a shilling a week by, and all the rest of her earnings should go to her. Mima, she said, must pay her something likewise; she got sadly too much money to do her good.

Finding her mother so reasonable, Letty ventured to ask how much money she already had, and whether she might put that in the Savings Bank?

"Your money is in the Savings Bank already," said her mother, meaning to be witty; "you need not be afraid—it's safe enough under lock and key," and, glancing towards the desk, she nodded her head.

"I should so like to know how much I have!" said Letty.

"I'll maybe tell you some day or other," said her mother, when I'm at my desk.

"Let me look now," said Letty, almost wondering at her own temerity; "I won't meddle with anything; you shall stand by, if you like, and see me all the time."

"I will trust nobody at my desk," replied Mrs. Higgins, angrily. "I've missed money of late, and a many other things from my desk."

"I never was at the desk!" exclaimed Letty—"never in all my life! When I was a child, how I used to long to know what was inside! I know there are some little drawers, and a pretty little door in the middle, and that's all."

Mima sat on one side the fire whilst this conversation went on, reading a pamphlet with a gaudily painted frontispiece. The pamphlet was called "The Tragical History of the Fair Maid of Valley," and

was greatly admired by all the seven-and-twenty girls
who worked in Warrington's mending-room; it was
going the round of the whole set now, and Rachel Ford
was to have it as soon as Mima Higgins had finished;
she was in the very heart of the story when her mother and sister began their conversation; she kept her
eyes fixed on the page, but she did not read one word
all the time they were talking. As soon as they had
done, she re-arranged herself in her chair, and addressed herself to go on with the book; but she could
not connect one word with another; there was something in what either her mother or Letty had said,
that quite discomposed her, so, closing the book, she
sat musing for awhile, and then said she would go and
ask Eliza Jones to take a walk with her; but whatever was passing in her mind, was between herself
and her own conscience, for neither her mother nor
Letty perceived any peculiarity about her.

It was a great pleasure to Letty to put by a shilling
a week in the Provident Society; she never before
felt so happy and so self-satisfied. She and Mr. Ford
at the next house, who had also just began to reserve
five shillings of his weekly wages for the Savings
Bank, could have sympathized with each other en-
tirely. The remembrance, or rather the consciousness
of her little hoard, made even sleep in her solitary
garret pleasant. There was a self-complacency in
the thought, a respectability in the circumstance of
having a something that she could call her own.

The ladies who came weekly on their domiciliary
visits, to collect the savings of the poor, would sit down
and talk for a quarter or half an hour with Letty and
Mrs. Greaseley; and soon it came to be a thing anti-
cipated with pleasure, from one week's end to another.
The hearth was swept up with more than common care,
two chairs set ready, and the card and the shilling laid
on the lace-frames ready, beside its respective owner.
The ladies that came into Bartram's Court talked

to the ladies who went into other courts, and compared notes, and agreed that nowhere, certainly, were there such respectable people as at Nos. 6 and 7, in this same Bartram's Court; but especially did they uphold the lodger in the chamber at No. 6, and the poor deformed girl of the house, who seemed so much attached, and yet were no relation to each other. Miss Phillips, one of the collectors for this district, would preach quite a homily about the virtues of the poor, taking for her text the two poor lace-workers at No. 6, Bartram's Court.

The regularity of Letty's life, the pleasant consciousness that she was laying by money, and the uniform, almost maternal kindness of Mrs. Greaseley, made her nearly forget that she was unlike everybody else. She went to church regularly, and, though she was not dressed like her sister, still she was, as her mother said, always neat and clean. She never had known till this winter, and this was the winter when distress began to cry, as it were, aloud in the streets, what real comfort of body and mind was. She had almost forgotten the money which her mother kept locked up in the desk; she might have forgotten it altogether, had it not been for one little occurrence, which we must relate.

It was her duty to straighten the bed-clothes in the lean-to, after Mima was gone to her work; her mother said, she made the bed badly, and therefore she need do no more than that; she herself would shake it when she came home at night. One morning, therefore, when she was engaged in these little duties, she was surprised beyond measure, to find her mother's keys hanging under the bed-clothes, caught, as it were, in a loose piece of the mattrass-binding, as if they had slipped out of her pocket, which she had, perhaps, laid on the bed, and, catching thus, had not fallen to the floor, and had not therefore been heard or seen. She could hardly believe her eyes; such a thing as this had, perhaps, never occurred before—perhaps never might occur again.

I 2

The keys! the long and anxiously-desired keys, were in her hand; let her use them as she would, she could never be discovered, for her mother finding them hanging where she herself had found them, would understand the accident, and never suspect their being removed. Again, the desire to open the desk, to see all that it contained, but above all, to know how much of her money her mother held in her hand, took possession of her mind. There could be no harm in doing so; it was altogether different to opening Mr. Greaseley's money-drawer. She remembered how Mrs. Greaseley had told her mother, that it was only natural she should like to look at her money sometimes. "I must see how much I have; Mrs. Greaseley herself would say, it was only natural!" argued she.

She looked at the door; the key was turned in the lock as usual, and, with a heart that beat almost as wildly as when she first opened Mr. Greaseley's money-drawer, she unlocked the desk, but as silently as if she had been a night-thief, lest Mrs. Greaseley above stairs should hear her; although, the moment before, she had made that good old woman authority for the action. She was too much agitated to think, when the desk lay open before her, of all the marvels and mysteries with which her childish fancy had invested it, but all in hurried trepidation opened first one, and then another little drawer, curious to know what really were their contents, and anxiously impatient to find some box, or purse, or bag, which might contain her money. The contents of these drawers were more multifarious than the contents of Mrs. Greaseley's little chest; but their contents were all worthless. Where were the silver spoons which she had seen so many years ago brought from that very desk? Where was her money, which her mother had assured her was safe there? Suppose, after all, it was her own money that her mother said she had missed. She grew

impatient to search yet farther.   There was a little
key in this little door in the centre—she opened it;
an old castor-stand, minus one foot, and holding only
a mustard-pot, stood within—the sole inhabitant, as
it fancifully seemed, of the little fairy palace which in
her childhood she had imagined it.

At that very moment a sound at the window startled her, and, looking up, she saw the face of Mima
above the window-blind; she tapped at the window and
laughed, Letty thought in triumph and derision.   The
sudden striking of a thunderbolt might have levelled
her to the earth at once, but it could not have given a
shock equal to that which the unexpected sight of her
sister at that moment occasioned.

"Oh, gracious God!" exclaimed she, suddenly closing the desk, and, without even stopping to lock it,
throwing the keys into the bedroom.   Mima knocked
and rattled at the door, and the voice of Mrs. Greaseley was heard through the window above, demanding
who was there.   It doubled her anguish to think of
her friend above stairs knowing a syllable of the affair:
so, to keep the evil as small as possible, mighty as it
was at the best, she opened the door and met her sister with a face crimson with guilty consciousness.

"So, Miss," began Mima, in a taunting voice, "I
have interrupted your studies—it's you that go and
take the old woman's money, is it?   I'm glad I've
found you out!"

"I never touched the money!   I have seen no
money now!" exclaimed Letty, trembling all over.

"Oh yes!" said Mima, "deny it! who expects anything else?   If I had not seen with my own eyes, now,
I should never have believed it, nor would you have
confessed it!"

"I never did open this desk before," exclaimed
Letty.   "What can I say to make you believe me?
This is the first time in all my life, I do assure
you!"

"You didn't open it this morning, eh!" said Mima, jeeringly.

"I wish I had not!" exclaimed Letty, almost in despair—"I wish I had never found the keys—I wish I had never touched them! Oh, what will mother say? she will almost kill me!" said she, wringing her hands.

"You did not expect me," said Mima, laughing; "my word, how you did jump!"

Letty made no answer, but began to cry bitterly.

"I know now," said Mima, "who took the money out of the desk—you had a famous opportunity, here all by yourself. I often wondered how you got all that money for your Provident Societies and Savings Banks! My word! what will mother say?"

Letty cried more than ever, and wrung her hands; at length, said she in a voice wonderfully calm for the state of agitation in which she was, "If I were lying on my death-bed, Mima, I should say what I say at this moment—I never did open the desk before this time; I found the keys lying on the bed, as they must have dropped from mother's pocket; my own money is in the desk; I don't know how much; mother has said, times without end, it was there, and by itself; there is a five-shilling piece and a half-sovereign amongst it, and I should know it if I found it; I wanted to know how much money there was—there was no harm in that, Mima! was there?"

"I dare say!" said Mima, in a tone intended to express that she did not believe a word of it.

"God in heaven knows!" exclaimed poor Letty, "that every syllable I have said is true; if I had found my own money I would not have taken one sixpence of it!"

"And you could not find it?" said Mima.

"No," replied Letty, "I found no money at all!"

"Very good!" said Mima, nodding her head, and looking as incredulous as possible, "perhaps the old

lady has taken it all away. But you know where it
ought to be; you have found money before now there,
you know!"

"Never! never!" exclaimed Letty; "how can you
say so, Mima?"

"What will mother say? what will Mrs. Greaseley
say?" said Mima.

"Mima!" exclaimed Letty, starting up from the low
seat on which she had thrown herself, " I am innocent—
God in heaven knows that I am innocent of taking
money from the desk—of ever having opened it before
this day; I have done wrong in so doing—I confess it!
but oh Mima!" said she, throwing herself on her knees
before her sister, "for Heaven's sake do not tell any one
what I have done! I am punished enough already!
All that I have in that desk, let it be whatever it may,
I will give you—only keep this secret. Oh! I would do
as much for you, and a deal more!"

"Well, get up then," said Mima, " and don't make
such a noise, or we shall have the old lady coming
down stairs."

" Every sixpence that mother has of mine," continued
Letty, rising from her knees, "I will give you; you
can say I have done so—it does not matter why! One
sister, you know, should be kind to another," added she,
bursting afresh into tears.

"Well, Letty," returned her sister, " that's all fair
enough, and what you say is true; I will keep the secret.
But mother will think it so odd about your giving me
your money: she'll suspect something, as sure as you're
alive! I'll tell you what you must do; you must give
me ten shillings out of your Provident Society money.
You can tell them you want to buy a cloak, for winter,
for I know they are very impertinent sort of folks, and
always will know how you spend every penny—that
made me never put in!"

Letty heaved a great sigh. " I have but nineteen
shillings in the Society," said she; "I have been more

than half a year in saving that—don't ask me for that money!"

"Very well," returned Mima, "then I'll tell mother everything!"

"Ask her," said Letty, "for my money out of the desk—she'll give it you; she never denies you anything; she'll ask you no questions; say I gave it you for love! There's more than ten shillings there—I know there is a five-shilling piece and a half-sovereign, besides odd shillings and sixpences!"

"That's a pretty come off," replied Mima; "I see plain enough that you don't mean to give me anything! Either ten shillings down, or I'll tell all!"

Letty groaned, while the tears ran down faster than ever.

"I see you don't mean to consent," said Mima; "then here goes!" and she began to tie her bonnet-strings, as if she would set off at once to her mother.

The stratagem succeeded; poor Letty, terrified almost out of her mind, promised to do whatever her sister required.

"And now, one thing more," said Mima; "you shall not say one word about giving me the ten shillings—neither to one creature nor to another; or if you do, I'll tell all the same as if you gave me not a penny!"

"What am I to do?" asked the unhappy and perplexed girl—"Mrs. Greaseley will want to know what I want ten shillings for!"

"Oh! you can manage her well enough," said Mima; "I could—that I know. Say you want shoes—anything! only this remember, if she know, why, then our agreement's at an end!"

Letty made no reply, but sate down again on the low seat, and covering her face with her hands, cried bitterly.

Mima also sate down by the fire, and, warming her handkerchief, put it to her cheek, saying she had the tooth-ache—that she had come home because it was so bad she could not work.

Letty did not hear a word that she said.

"And so you rummaged the desk through," said Mima, after she had sate some time warming her cheek; "come, tell me; I won't betray you—upon my word I won't!"

Letty looked up and asked her sister what she had said.

Mima repeated her words, adding, "Come, lend me the keys now; mother has lots of pretty things, I know, in the desk, and I should so like to see them! Just give me the keys, Letty, and I'll try to find your money. I'll be honourable, upon my word, and I'll tell you exactly how much you have! Come, child, don't be stupid; where are the keys?" repeated Mima, getting up from her chair; "we may as well be hanged for a sheep as for a lamb. Where are the keys, Letty? give them to me."

"I haven't got them," said Letty; "and pray, for Heaven's sake, do not open it again! Oh do not! do not!" exclaimed she, looking quite desperate—"you know how wrong it is!"

"Where are they?" demanded Mima, angrily.

"Somewhere in the bedroom," said Letty; "but indeed you shall not!" exclaimed she, rising with energy and holding her back.

Letty's strength was vain against her sister's, and Mima bursting from her, rushed into the bedroom, and returned the moment after, holding up the bunch of keys in triumph.

"For shame, Mima!" said Letty, filled with burning indignation, "to make me pay you ten shillings out of my little, that you may not tell of me, and you go and do the very same thing before my face!—Suppose I should tell of you?"

"That you dare not!" said Mima, with bitter scorn; "for your life, you dare not!"

"I'll not see you do it, then," said Letty, "I'll go!"

"You'll not dare to tell Mrs. Greaseley!" said Mima, catching her by the arm and holding her back,

as she was laying her hand on the staircase-door; "if
you do, I'll tell mother of you, as sure as you are
alive, and tell her also, that it's you that have taken
her money!"

"Let me go!" said Letty, again crying.

"Not till you promise me, on your soul," returned
her sister.

"I do promise!" said the poor Letty.

Letty did not go into Mrs. Greaseley's room, but up
into her own garret, and then, dropping on her knees,
she buried her face in the covering of her bed.

"I do repent! I do repent! God be merciful to me
a sinner!" were the only thoughts she uttered; for a
dead weight of guilt and misery seemed to press her
down to the very dust.

Mima in the mean time, troubling herself neither
about the little drawers, nor the little door in the middle, went direct to a secret deposit which she had visited
before then, leaving all exactly, to appearance, as it
was, went into the bedroom, and hung the keys in the
loose binding of the mattrass, precisely as Letty had
found them, and then went back to the warehouse,
finding, as we may suppose, her tooth-ache much
better.

Letty was greatly surprised when she found the
keys hanging just as they were at first; she fancied,
therefore, she must have told Mima how they were,
and yet she could not recall having done so. "But,
dear me," thought the poor, simple-hearted girl, "what
can I remember? I had scarcely sense left to put one
word to another—I dare say I did tell her!"

Very early in the evening, much earlier than usual,
Mrs. Higgins returned from her washing; Letty opened
the door, no little terrified lest this unusual circumstance had reference to her misdeed. Her mother,
however, took no notice of her, but went directly to
the sleeping-room; Letty heard her hastily turn over
the bed-clothes, and, discovering the keys, disengage

them, and drop them, the next moment, into her capacious pocket.

She did not say a word to Letty about them, but seemed in rather a remarkably good humour. So far the poor girl thought all was right. She had missed her keys during her washing, and hurried through it with more speed than common, to return home in search of them, and, having found what Letty herself supposed to be the fact, that in the night they had slipped from her pocket and thus secured themselves, became easy in her own mind.

Mima did not return home till late; she said, she and Eliza Jones had been home with one of their girls to New Radford, and, in coming back, had been to see the wax-works in the Exchange Rooms, which had been there ever since the fair. She, like her mother, seemed in a very good humour, and persuaded her to let them have a "bit of toasted cheese" for supper. She said Letty never tasted anything good, and if her mother would let them have it, she would tell them all she had seen, for the wax-work figures were all as big as life, and just like life, for all the world. She said Eliza Jones had asked one wax gentleman to be so good as to let her pass! Oh, it was so funny! she said; she thought they must contrive that Letty should see it—she had half a mind to treat her herself!

They had the toasted cheese for supper; and then, when it was ready, was ever such a piece of extravagance known at No. 6, before! Mrs. Higgins said they should have a pint of ale amongst them; so Mima, with threepence and a jug in her hand, and without her bonnet, ran off to the Ruben's Head to fetch it.

Mima told Letty, the next morning at breakfast, that it was all on her account that she had persuaded their mother to let them have such a nice supper; and she would see how kind she would be to her, if she were only a good girl.

к

Poor Letty wondered in her own mind all day, what it was that constituted being a good girl.

CHAPTER IX.

THE HERR DONNERUNDBLITZ'S GRAND NIGHT.

"SOMETHING very strange has come over you of late, Letty," said Mrs. Greaseley to her, the next Monday afternoon, as they two sate together as usual working their lace; "something very extraordinary—something quite beyond my understanding, Letty! and now, instead of putting the shilling by, you want nine shillings out! I'm sure there's something very wrong about this."

Letty made no reply—she did not know what to say; so, after Mrs. Greaseley had worked another sprig in the veil, she took off her spectacles and began again.

"Now, Letty, I really must know what all this means. You have looked poorly for several days, and have hardly spoken a word: something is on your mind! You have no business with secrets at your age; secrets are bad things, Letty, and so are mysteries of all kinds. Come, be a good girl, and tell me what is amiss, and in what you would spend this money; a young girl like you has no business to be spending ten shillings at a time, without being able to give any account of it."

"I'm not going to spend it," said she, in a low voice.

"Then what are you going to do with it?" asked Mrs. Greaseley.

Letty made no reply.

"Do you hear what I say?" asked the other.

Still Letty was silent.

"Well, Letty," said Mrs. Greaseley, "if you are going to sulk, and to make mysteries and secrets, I've

done. with you. I've not deserved this from you,
Letty," said she, in a tone of voice that showed she
was much hurt; " I have always been kinder to you,
even than your own mother!"

" That you have !" exclaimed Letty, bursting into
tears, " and I love you better than any creature in the
world. I often wish I was your servant—that I do!"
said the poor girl, sobbing bitterly.

Mrs. Greaseley herself began to cry.

"I'm sure," said Letty, " as soon as she could again
command her voice sufficiently to speak, " I wish I
could tell you—but indeed, indeed I dare not !"

Mrs. Greaseley's curiosity was more excited than
ever; she wiped her eyes and began to think. " Oh,
I know what it is," said she in a moment or two—
" Mima has got this money from you ! "

Letty cared not that Mrs. Greaseley should know
the truth; she feared Mima and her mother, far more
than she feared a falsehood. She did not, however,
think at that moment either about truth or falsehood—
she only thought of her sister's threat.

" No!" said she, but in a voice of extremest agitation—" Mima has nothing to do with it—but I can't
tell you a word about it !"

" I don't think you would tell me a lie," said Mrs.
Greaseley, struck, nevertheless, with Letty's guilty manner;" why should you ?—so I will believe you; but
nothing in all the world shall persuade me, if it is
not Mima, that it is not your mother !"

Letty thought there could be no great harm in Mrs.
Greaseley entertaining this belief; so she did not con-
tradict it.

" I knew I should find it out, Letty," said the other,
"and I'm glad I have; and now let me tell you, Letty,
that you have no business to take this money out, even
for your mother. Was it not her own promise, that if
you gave her all the rest, she would let you put in

the shilling a-week? She has no business to touch a
penny of this money," said the good woman, in a tone
of anger very unusual to her.

" Oh, I must have it out!" exclaimed Letty; " you
don't understand—indeed you don't; but I must have
it out!"

" Your mother cannot think of what she is doing,"
said Mrs. Greaseley; " I shall tell her about it, Letty,
as sure as you are born."

" You must not say a word about it!" exclaimed the
girl, starting up from her seat and catching her friend
by the arm—" not a word—not a syllable: you must
not even think about it," said she, in a hurried, terrified
voice; "not a single syllable must you breathe to her;
she would almost kill me if you did!" and the poor
girl, having far more to conceal, and far more cause
for fear than her friend, by any possibility, could con-
ceive, burst into a passion of tears.

" You need not fear," said Mrs. Greaseley, kindly,
and quite touched by her distress; " but I am more
angry with your mother than I can tell. Is she not
satisfied with having got all your money for above a
year, not one farthing of which you will ever see, but
she must compel you, under what threat and what pretence I cannot tell, to get from you more than half of
your savings?"

Letty still continued to cry, and her friend pro-
ceeded:—

" I know it would be very wrong in me to set a
child against its mother; but I must speak my mind.
If your mother, Letty, was old and infirm, or even if
she was sickly, or had any plea whatever to set up, it
would be so different—but she has none; and getting
your money in this way is no better than robbery : you
might just as well take her keys and break into her
desk, and steal her money! I haven't patience with
her—a hard-hearted, selfish, sordid woman! But every-

body knows her; and, if it were not for your sake, Letty, I'd go out—that I would."

There was a deal in this long speech of Mrs Greaseley's, which made poor Letty almost writhe; nor yet had she courage to set her friend right: she merely repeated, that "she wished she could tell her all; and that, indeed, indeed she must have the money."

"I'll tell you what you shall do from this time forth," said Mrs. Greaseley; "you shall only put sixpence a week by in your own name—the other sixpence shall go with my money; you may depend upon me—that you may. I could not find in my heart to wrong you of one farthing; more shame on your mother, who would, as it were, rob her own child, and she no better than a cripple!" Mrs. Greaseley wiped her eyes, for she loved Letty, and had wrought herself up into a state of deep sympathy with her.

Letty sighed—nay, almost groaned, for she thought she did not deserve all this kindness; and that, if Mrs. Greaseley found out how she had deceived her, how grieved and angry she also would be.

"Oh, here are the ladies!" exclaimed she, the next moment, seeing them turn into the court. "Do not say a word to them about it—do not! do not!" repeated she, clasping the old woman's arm almost convulsively, and fearing that this web of sophistry, in which, as it were, she was so unexpectedly caught, was not strong enough to sustain her.

"No, I won't," said Mrs. Greaseley; "but still, I do think your mother should be spoken to; and the ladies could do it so naturally."

"Not for Heaven's sake!" exclaimed the girl, almost beside herself with terror; "mother would kill me if she knew!"

The ladies seemed nearly as much surprised, and as reluctant as Mrs. Greaseley herself. They said it was a pity Letty should want her money; they said a deal about economy; about young women commonly laying

out all their money in dress; they said, they hoped
Letty was not going to follow her sister's example, and
a great deal more; adding, that the working-classes
ought now to begin rigidly to save, for that it was
everybody's opinion, that such a time of distress was
approaching as had never been known in the memory
of man.   They said that Westons and Warringtons
both, would only be able to give their hands work
three days in the week, and that, next, week even a
reduction of wages was spoken of; and in conclusion,
they again urged the necessity of economy and self-
denial, and inquired if, after this, Letty would take
out so much money: they advised her not, if she
wanted it merely for dress; if her mother needed it,
they said, that was another thing, for children must
always assist their parents.

Mrs. Greaseley looked with a very peculiar expression, and said it was a great shame if Mrs. Higgins
wanted money, seeing she neither was in bad health,
nor was she in want of employment.   Mrs. Higgins
ought to be ashamed, she said, if she could not save
money herself.

Letty was frightened almost beyond knowing what
she did, for she thought Mrs. Greaseley was going to
tell them; so she said, she did not want the money for
her mother, but that, nevertheless, she must have it!"

"Letty," said Mrs. Greaseley, as soon as the ladies
were gone, "it was very wrong of you to tell a point-
blank lie about what you wanted the money for!"

"I thought you were going to tell them," said the
poor girl, feeling like a miserable wretch struggling
deeper and deeper in the bog into which one false
step has plunged her.   "I thought you were going to
tell them that mother wanted the money; and then, if
they had talked to her, what in the world would have
become of me?"

"Well, child, remember this," said Mrs. Greaseley,
feeling sorry for her, but thinking it her duty to be

angry, "that whatever I had said, you had no right to
tell a lie; and if ever I hear you do so again, Letty,
I'll never let you come into my room. I never will
forgive you—and so now you know!"

"Oh dear, dear, what will become of me?" said poor
Letty, beginning again to cry, and wishing that she
dared confess to Mrs. Greaseley everything, even to
looking into her husband's money-drawer; and then,
thought she, "if I dared only do that, how happy I
should be! and I never, never again, would tell one
falsehood, or do one thing which would displease
her!"

She received the nine shillings from her little hoard,
and with the one she reserved this week, gave them
to Mima.

"You saw what a nice supper I got for you the
other night," said her sister; "and, if you are a good
girl, I'll get you many a treat. There are going to be
fireworks at Radford Folly—you never saw fireworks
in all your life!—you'd like to go, wouldn't you? It's
only sixpence a piece; and, ten to one, when you get
there, somebody will treat you; somebody will treat
me, that I know!"

"Who?" said Letty, thinking her sister's manner
solicited the question.

"Then, never tell; as sure as you are alive, never
tell!" said Mima, "why, my beau—that's Charles
Hearson; they call him 'Curly,' because he's such
handsome hair—oh, such a nice young man! There'll
be a dance, and lots of fun. I wouldn't miss going for
the world!"

"I should like to go," said Letty.

"You can't go with us, however," rejoined her
sister. "'Liza Jones goes with her beau: we shall sail on
the lake, and there'll be music, and all so grand! I
thought I'd tell you, Letty—arn't you obliged to me?"

"I should so like to go!" said poor Letty.

"You must persuade the old woman up stairs to go;

she and you can walk about quietly and look on—there'll be plenty of fun!"

All the working world of Nottingham talked of the great evening's entertainment at Radford Folly, or Grove, as it was called in the newspaper advertisements, and in the placards, red, blue, and yellow, that were posted at the corners of every street. "Only sixpence a-piece, and children half-price," said many a father and mother, who wished to go—and yet counted the cost—"only sixpence a-piece—that's not much!"

The man who exhibited the fireworks was a German: he had, a week before, made "a grand exhibition" in the market-place, and had collected for his remuneration, as he would say, "nach belieben," or what you please to give; and now, professing himself grateful to the "nobility and gentry of the place," solicited their patronage of a "Grand Entertainment, to be concluded by Fireworks, in the delicious Gardens of Radford Grove." Herr Donnerundblitz declared to the master of the Radford Grove Coffee House, that his gardens were quite a little Prater, and might be made the most attractive place in the world. There was not, therefore, a single house in any street, lane, court, or road, into which one of the celebrated Herr Donnerundblitz's circulars was not sent. "Gardens to be opened at 6 o'clock precisely; admission only sixpence; children under twelve years, half-price.

People forgot, for the moment, the troubles of the day, and everywhere nothing was talked of but fireworks and the gardens of Radford Folly.

"A thousand pities," said Miss Phillips, and other collectors for the Provident Society, that these people come here with their dissipations for the poor; we shall find, next Monday, that greater part of our depositors have nothing!"

"I wish to goodness these Germans would keep away, with their fireworks and nonsense," said many a little shopkeeper, whose day-book was full of poor creditors, " it is not the poor in the long run who will pay for this night's folly, but such as we, who might otherwise have received, as part payment, the sixpence, or shilling, or half-crown, that will be spent! "

" I'm sure we can't afford to go," said also many a prudent poor father and mother of a family; "but bless me! if we are to wait till we can afford it, we may never have a bit of pleasure all the days of our lives; so we'll e'en make a push, just this once, and go ! "

" I'll go, sure enough," said Mrs. Jones, who was grown quite reckless, "for 'Liza will go, and so will Jones; so I'll take that other blanket and pawn it; it's not so very cold yet, and they can lay their clothes on the bed ! I and the two children will go; for, Heaven help us! one never sees a bit of life in this court, from one week's end to another ! "

" Don't you think you can afford to go ? " said Ford to his wife, just for once; " there's no great harm done; and I'll give the five shillings myself, instead of putting it by this week."

Mrs. Ford demurred, but did not refuse.

" I'll have the pleasure of treating you all—that I will," said he; and then he counted up on his fingers how many they were; " it will only cost two and ninepence; and the two and threepence we'll spend when we are there; we'll have coffee and a quart of ale; we'll make a night of it just for once! It is not often," continued he, "that we take a bit of pleasure together; and when I'm there, with you leaning on my arm, and all the children about me, Lord! I shall feel like a man ! "

His wife felt the affectionate compliment, and said, " Oh yes, they would go ! "

" Don't say a word to the children about it," said Ford; " they shall think they are not going, I'll be so cross to them if they say anything about going; it will only make the pleasure the greater at last;" and poor Ford rubbed his hands at the idea of the little joke.

" Won't you go to the fireworks ? " said Mima Hig-

gins to her mother; "as it will be on a Friday you may
as well, and take Letty with you."

"All stuff and nonsense!" said Mrs. Higgins; I
don't get my money so easy as that. If Letty likes
to go, well and good—but I shall stay at home; there'll
be fools enough without me!"

"I should so like to go!" said Letty to Mrs.
Greaseley, on the Thursday as they two sate together
at their work, "just for once: should you not like it?"

"Oh child! I really care nothing about such things,"
replied Mrs. Greaseley; "I'm an old woman and a
bad walker, and it's damp there; and if my asthma gets
bad before winter, what's to become of me?"

Letty was bent upon going; and all her friend's
arguments about economy, which she frequently made
use of, were of no avail.

"What's the use of living," said Letty, if one is never
to enjoy one's self? Do you know, I get so tired of
always stopping at home, and day after day sitting and
working, working, that I don't know what to do! I've
set my mind on going to-morrow, and go I certainly
must, even if it cost me two shillings."

"Rather than you should make such a trouble about
it," said Mrs. Greaseley, who perhaps, after, all, was
not displeased with this excuse for going, "I'll go if
I'm pretty well to-morrow." But one thing you shall
promise me," said her friend, "you shall not again
spend your money in this sort of folly; once in awhile
is quite enough."

"No, I'll never ask you to go again as long as you
live," said Letty.

There came then as much discussion as to what
should be worn, as if they had been ladies of fashion
going to a court-ball. Letty wanted her friend to put
on the printed gown, which, above all others, was her
admiration, with a crimson spun silk shawl; but the old
lady herself was resolutely bent upon her snuff-
coloured bombazine, and her old-fashioned scarlet

cloth cloak, which, on account of the damp and her asthma, was much more suitable. The garments lay abroad in the chamber the next morning, and Letty, as usual, was deeply impressed with a sense of the lodger's wealth in wearing apparel.

"Well, Letty, as you admire the shawl so much," said Mrs. Greaseley, "you shall wear it to-night; it will look a deal smarter, I grant you, than your old plaided one."

Again the girl was overjoyed and filled with unspeakable gratitude; she put it on in anticipation, and as she folded her arms in its soft, silken amplitude, was filled with the agreeable sense of looking very respectable. "And I'll tell you what I'll do," continued Mrs. Greaseley, "I'll give you the printed gown for your very own—that I will!" said she, seeing Letty almost speechless—"I'm only an old woman, and I've no children to come after me; it will make you a nice Sunday-frock."

"Oh, how pretty it is!" exclaimed Letty, hanging it over the back of a chair, to get the effect of it; "oh dear, how obliged to you I am?"

"Does Mrs. Ford at the next house make gowns?" asked Mrs. Greaseley.

Letty did not know; she thought not. "We'll ask her," said Mrs. Greaseley; "and if not, we can maybe manage it ourselves."

The girl was overjoyed, and was trying to express her gratitude, when Mrs. Greaseley, rising suddenly from her chair, went to the window, saying somebody was at the door. "Well to be sure! who would have thought it!" exclaimed she, "Letty, run down and open the door."

Letty did as she was bid, and found there Mrs. Smith, Mrs. Greaseley's sister, who lived at Thrumpton, eight miles off.

Letty knew her, for she came now and then.

Mrs. Greaseley seemed very glad to see her, and

asked Letty to go and fetch a pint of ale; and began immediately to spread a cloth on the table, preparatory to reaching out the bread and cheese. Letty's first thought was, that perhaps Mrs. Smith's coming would prevent their going to the Folly that evening; but the next moment, all apprehension was removed. She said that she was come to see the fire-works that night; that her son had driven her over in their little cart, and she hoped to persuade her sister to go with them. She said her son would have no nay, although, for an old body like her, it was all a pack of nonsense. Mrs. Greaseley said she thought the same, but that, nevertheless, she had made up her mind to go—people could not always stay moping at home. Presently Mrs. Smith's son John came, and then Letty had to fetch another pint of ale, although John protested he had both eaten and drank at the Ruben's Head the minute before.

Letty was very bashful before the Smiths ; so, after she had done all she could to be useful, she rolled up the pretty printed gown and took it to her own garret, where, putting it on, although a world too long and large, she had the pleasure of admiring herself in it, through the tiny piece of broken looking-glass before which she daily performed her toilet.

All Bartram's Court was astonished to see the little cart painted green, with two or three chairs in it, and drawn by a bright bay frisking pony, driven about four o'clock up to Mrs. Higgin's door. Mima, who was dressing in the lean-to, and who had had a glimpse already of young Mr. Smith, came out with only three hooks of her frock fastened behind, and a pink handkerchief over her shoulders, to see them go off. Mr. Smith, however, was unfortunately too busy with the pony, which he called "a vicious toad," to notice her; so, spite of her pink handkerchief and long curls, the three being comfortably seated in the cart, he mounted to the board in front, and away they went, almost cantering out of the court, whilst Mrs. Higgins, who was bringing in her clothes from the line, nodded to them without smiling. Ford, who had carried on his joke, though it was but a poor one, to the very last, stood at his door in a capital humour. He had five shillings in his pocket, which he had that morning got from the foreman in advance of his wages, and he made the baby laugh and crow, and almost leap out of his arms, while he trotted it, in imitation of the cantering pony. At last, all were ready, and Mrs. Ford, putting her arm within her husband's off they set, as happy a family that day, as any in Nottingham. Rachel tapped, as they went out, at Mrs. Higgins's window, to let Mima know that she was gone, and then paused a moment at the Joneses, to see if Eliza was there; but the door was fastened and all were gone; and then, at the court end, nodded to a young man who stood there, and who, she told her sister, was a particular friend of Mima's—Charles, or as he was commonly called, Curly Hearson—did not she think him handsome? Jane said, she did not like the look of him, and that he was a man who would make her afraid.

Never in all her life had Letty Higgins conceived anything equal to these gardens; she had never heard of the Gardens of Hesperides, nor of the Gardens of Armida; but she had heard of the Garden of Eden, and this she thought must be like it. Hundreds of people were there, some walking about, some seated under the trees, drinking and smoking, and talking; young men were swinging girls in the swings fastened between two tall trees; children were playing at hide and seek among the bushes; and everywhere there was laughing and loud talking. There was a tall wooden erection at the end of the garden, where they said the fireworks were to be, and men with high ladders were yet busily employed, nailing on laths and slight timbers. To Letty it seemed all like a fairy-land; there was a little lake in the middle of the gardens, on which people

L

sailed gaily about in a brightly-painted boat, or landed on the little island in the middle, where stood a sort of Chinese temple, painted green and white, from under the umbrella-like roof of which, people shouted and made merriment with those who sailed below. The sun shone on the smooth closely shorn grass; the flower-beds were trim and neat, and filled with hundreds of splendidly coloured dahlias; everybody said the gardens looked pretty; no wonder, therefore, at Letty's enthusiasm.

There was plenty of tea and co had, and everywhere was to be h and saucers, and a jingling of on and smiled, and smiled too she could lay the smallest cl She saw the Fords come i smiled at them, and at poor miserable children; and at ticular friend," and a grou ran screaming and laughin

Presently, the two old and must go and sit dow room of the coffee-house, ting beside, and said t Greaseley said, they wo Letty should thus drin was ordered and broug then Mrs. Smith produc a-dozen slices of excell time over their tea, an while Letty looked th in the room, at what then, when tea was a pint of wine, to b which her son, who to drink. Mrs. Sm , carried on a a little, a little money to spend. She didn't often come to the town, she said, but when she did, she liked to make herself comfortable. Letty thought she was the most munificent woman in the world.

When the wine was finished, the two old ladies said they must go once more into the gardens to see what was going on, and then come in again before the room got crowded, and take their station at one of the windows, to see the fireworks.

The number of people by this time had greatly increased; the swings were all occupied, and a fiddler was playing merrily, while about forty couple were dancing. Everywhere people were drinking and smoking, and seeming full of enjoyment. Who, looking on, would have thought that distress—pinching, grinding distress—was among these people? Letty again saw the Joneses and the Fords, with whom the Dunnets seemed to have joined in a family group; and there—Letty could hardly believe her eyes—was her mother, dressed up in her Sunday things, walking about with a fat, tawdry-dressed acquaintance of hers, one Mrs. Ward.

As it grew dusk, the number of men who came without their families, straight from forge and factory, in their working clothes, greatly increased. An attentive observer would not have been long without perceiving something peculiar about these men; they were not come there alone for pleasure; some leading and powerful interest was operating among them, quite independent of fireworks and merriment. They stood together apart, and in groups, and talked eagerly and angrily; then some emissary, dispatched from among them, would be seen threading the idle groups in which women and children were mingled, singling out some individual, tapping him on the shoulder, or giving him some sign which he understood, and taking him along with them. Such a one came to the group where Ford was standing, and beckoned him away. "It won't do any longer," said the man to him, "we are all in a mind now, and shall strike for wages on Monday morning." Ford said, "Yes, something must be done." "On Monday morning," said Jones of Bartram's Court," who was holding forth to the group towards which Ford was led, "On Monday morning, every mother's son among them would strike for wages.", "Let's strike terror into them at once—we don't go to the root of the thing," said Curly Hearson. "Hush! Hearson, not so loud," said another; "we'll strike first for five days' employment in the week, or a rise in wages."

"Have you heard," said a third, who was just come from the town, and who, by his being out of breath, appeared to have been running, "have you heard that it's all up with Westons?" "With Westons!" exclaimed Ford.

"Lawyers are in the warehouse," said the man; "Westons won't do another stroke of business; they are done for, sure enough."

"You must all come to the coffee-house," said a man, who just came up and addressed the whole group; "Orator Timmins will read a letter of his to the Secretary for Home Affairs, on the state of the people. The Review won't give it; so he wants you all to hear it."

Everybody adjourned to the coffee-house, and were so deep in political discussions, that the little cannon had been fired the third time, and the fireworks had actually commenced, before the People's Association, as they called themselves, became aware of the circumstance; and then, all at once jumping up, and crowding to the windows, almost annihilated poor Mrs. Greaseley, her sister, and Letty, who had squeezed themselves, notwithstanding, into the smallest possible space; and, not till good Mrs. Greaseley had remonstrated at least a dozen times, "Please, sir, lift up your foot—oh dear, you tread on my gown," did she succeed, and that only at the expense of a rent of a quarter of a yard long, in gathering the snuff-coloured bombazine about her.

Letty heard people on all hands say, the fireworks were not good—that they were nothing to those in the market-place—that their pockets had fairly been picked—and that they would go and give the German Herr a blowing up, with other similar disparaging remarks, all of which filled her with astonishment; for to her it seemed that nothing in this world could have been half so beautiful, or half so grand before.

" Now John, do be steady; remember what a beast that pony is," said Mrs. Smith, as, about ten o'clock, they drove away from the gardens; and then, while John, who had drank rather more glasses than common, drove as steadily as he could, his mother told her sister and Letty what an impish creature was the pony, and how she knew, some day or other, it would be the death of somebody.

When they got home, they found Mrs. Higgins just returned; she was in a very odd sort of humour, and looked very odd too, and Letty thought, though she did not hint her thoughts to Mrs. Greaseley, that surely she must be tipsy.

CHAPTER X.

WHAT CAME AFTER PLEASURE, AND A SCENE IN THE POLICE OFFICE.

THE next morning, scarcely had Letty and Mrs. Greaseley sate down to their lacework, when the little green car, but not drawn by the bay pony of yesterday, again drove up to Mrs. Higgins's door. The moment young Mr. Smith entered his aunt's room, he broke out into vehement indignation against all ponies in general, and against his pony in particular, and told how that, on their way home the night before, one or two other

L 2

carts being behind them, the pony set off at full gallop,
when the driver of one of the other carts wishing to
pass, of all places in the world, chose a bridge for
that purpose; that their wheel was caught in that of the
passing cart, which occasioned his mother to be thrown
out and her leg unfortunately broken. He had him
self, he said, ridden off for the doctors, who were then
with her; and that he was now come to ask, as a great
favour, his aunt to go back with him, just to stay till
the worst was over. Poor Mrs. Greaseley was over-
whelmed, and thrown into the utmost perplexity by
this sad intelligence. Her husband would be at home
the next day—how could she go? and yet her sister,
ill and wanting her presence, how could she refuse?

Letty said she would make the fire that night for
Mr. Greaseley, and have everything as orderly and
comfortable as if she herself were at home; and, if she
might but be trusted, how happy she should be!

Mrs. Greaseley deliberated a long time, during which
her nephew and Letty used their utmost efforts to persuade her to go, and at length succeeded. " Well,
Letty," said she, " now pay particular attention—the
key of the corner cupboard I take off the bunch, and
leave in the door—the bunch I hang up within the
cupboard. You must explain all to him when he
comes home—you must tell him, child too, why I went
to Thrumpton; and mind and don't light the fire
till he comes into the court, or he'll think there's a
danger of fire, as there would be, and a waste of coal
too; and don't stand dawdling about the room when
you've done your two or three odd jobs—that wouldn't
please him; and mind above all things, always to keep
the chamber door locked when he's gone, and the key
on the ledge above the door!" These orders, and a
many others, being given, Mrs. Greaseley made what
hasty preparations were necessary, and accompanied
her nephew.

Letty, full of sorrow and sympathy for the kind old

woman, who had ended her little excursion of pleasure
so terribly, set about tidying her friend's room, raking
out the old ashes, and laying a fresh fire to be lighted
when Mr. Greaseley returned.   Her lace-frame she
raised against the wall, as it was placed on a Sunday,
for she made up her mind not to work again that day.
" I won't touch the bunch of keys," said she to herself,
" nor even open the cupboard door, unless Mr. Greaseley tells me; nor will I do any one single thing that
she would not like! "   She kept a careful look-out for
Mr. Greaseley in the evening, and as soon as she saw
him approaching the house, went up stairs and lit his
fire.   Her mother told him below stairs of the accident which had occurred, and he, instead of sympa-
thising, as she expected, grew very angry, and said
he wondered what business old women like them had
going to fireworks, either at one Folly or another; and
then came tramping so heavily up stairs, that Letty
was quite frightened.   She delivered her message respecting the keys, and then asked, as modestly and
properly as she knew how, if she should set out his
supper and fetch him his pint of ale?   He did not say
she might; but, as he went out of the house about half-
an-hour afterwards, and did not return till ten, she supposed he had taken his supper at the public house.
The next morning she made his bed, as she had promised; and, as he did not come in till night, the Higginses concluded he had been to Thrumpton.
     On Monday morning Mima returned from the
warehouse, about an hour after she had gone there:
there was a strike for wages, she said, and nobody was
allowed to work; such being the case, she didn't care
if she helped her sister that day, and so Letty couldn't
call her ill-natured.   Letty was quite pleased with her
offer, and the two went up stairs to bring the frame
down. Letty asked her sister, if she did not think everything very neat and nice? for she had put all in order

that morning. Mima went into the bedroom and peeped about, and said, "what lots of things the Greaseleys had—but nothing to the Fords. Rachel Ford," she said, "had taken her up stairs and shown her worlds of things!" Letty was a little piqued by the idea of the Fords' possessions being richer than her friend's, and she began to boast of the various wealth of all the locked-up places; but, talking of Mrs. Greaseley's things, Letty said she would show her sister what a pretty gown she had given her.

It was always a difficult thing for Letty to go up stairs; so, when she was there, she thought she would make her bed, and save herself the trouble of going a second time. Mima thus had an opportunity to turn the key in the corner-cupboard, and take a survey of its contents. Letty, quite unconscious of what had been done in her absence, displayed, on her return, her present with exultation.

"Has she many such gowns as these?" asked Mima.

Letty, proud of her old friend's wardrobe, began to tell, a second time, what each chest of drawers and box contained.

"And what's in this drawer?" asked Mima, pointing to the one containing Mr. Greaseley's Sunday clothes, which Letty had passed over. After a deal of teazing persuasion, she told her sister, and why there was such a mystery attached to it—the key of his money-drawer was kept in his waistcoat-pocket; but as to where his money-drawer was, that was a secret she dared not tell for her life. Mima asked her no more, but said, that as this room was so much lighter and more cheerful than the one below, they might just as well work there, for that nobody would know. Letty, however, was resolute not to do so; she had promised, she said, to keep the door locked, and all neat and orderly, and that she would do: the frame, therefore, was carried down stairs. Mima worked for about half an hour, and then, seeing Eliza Jones in the yard, went out to her, and did not return till night.

That day, the court was visited by a deputation of the turn-out hands, who were paying domiciliary visits, forbidding any frame-working, or lace-work of any kind being done, and threatening that, after this warning, any person who should persist in working, would have his frame broken, and his work destroyed. The lady-collectors of the Provident Society, too, made their round, and great was their surprise, and not light their displeasure, to find Letty and the good old lodger so signally delinquent. Wherever they went that day, they found discontent and fermentation. "It was a shocking thing, this strike for wages," said the ladies; "it always must end in increased distress; and there was not, besides, a manufacturer in the town who could afford to raise his wages; the poor must be contented to suffer with society generally; and why, they would ask, had everybody flocked to Radford Folly last Friday, and spent so much money there?"

There was no one poor family this Monday afternoon, to whom this visit was welcome: the ladies were angry, and the poor were angry likewise, while the terrible news of the certain failure of the Westons cast a gloom over the town, like the outspread wings of some angel of judgment. There was a distrust and a spirit of opposition and revolt abroad, which many feared; and it was generally believed, that the struggle between the two parties would this time be long and terrible. The masters said, that they, for their parts, would take it quietly; they had already too large stocks of goods, and could afford to wait; the men said, that if they died in the streets they would not again come in to work on the same terms; and that they had power in their hands, of which the masters had no idea. Such being the state of things, a general holiday prevailed, but by no means a holiday of pleasure and rest.

One day Letty sate with the printed gown on her
knee, wishing, now that she had nothing to do, she
could only make it up, when Mima came in and volunteered to help her, saying, that if she would begin to
pick it to pieces, she would go in and borrow a pattern
from Rachel Ford, for all the Fords made their own
things. Never was poor Letty so grateful to her sister before; it was a long time, however, before Mima
came back, and then she came full of news. The
Fords, she said, were in a pretty taking; that he had lost
all his Savings Bank money through Mr. Weston; and
there he was, cursing and swearing, and going on like
a madman; she knew he had been quite drunk the
night before, and people said he had been fighting; he
had a black eye this morning, and she should not wonder if it were so; and Mrs. Ford was crying so as
nothing was like it. She had not got the pattern,
therefore, she said, but as she and Eliza Jones and
Rachel were going in the afternoon to Wilford, she
would ask her, and that, in the meantime, they would
sit down and unpick it; and " now, what will you give
me for working at this frock till it is done ?" asked she.

" Oh, I havn't anything to give," said Letty, frightened lest her sister wanted more money; " you know
I have so very little."

" Well, poor thing !" returned the other, " I won't
ask for anything; only tell me again, what the old
folks have up stairs; you don't know, Letty, how I like
to hear you talk—it's as good as a fairy-tale; and I'm
sure they must be very rich: I shouldn't wonder if the
old fellow is a miser;" and then Mima began to tell her
poor simple sister all kinds of rhodomontading stories
about misers and their locked-up hoards, till her imagination was in complete excitement; and, unsuspicious
of her sister's artifices, she told of the curious old-
.fashioned chest and its mysterious drawer.

All that morning Mima helped her; in the afternoon, she went to Wilford, but not, as she had said,

with Rachel Ford.   After that day, she said no more
about assisting to make the new frock, and when Letty
inquired if she had got the pattern, she said she had
forgotten it, but would remember it next time.

Nothing could exceed the order in which Letty kept
the two rooms; every day she dusted all that they contained; and on the two nights when Mr. Greaseley slept
at home, as he said nothing to the contrary, she believed
him perfectly satisfied with her little housewifery.
During the whole of the week, too, she never once
even turned the key in the corner cupboard door, and
scrupulously kept the key of the chamber door on the
ledge above it; so that she felt happy in having, as
she believed, performed her duties to the letter.

On Saturday morning the little green cart and
sober horse brought back Mrs. Greaseley; her sister
was wonderfully well, considering the accident and her
time of life; and the good old woman came back in the
most cheerful of tempers.

The next morning, just about breakfast time, the
family of the Higginses heard above stairs a most
extraordinary noise: Mr. Greaseley was in a tremen-
dous passion, and heavy steps were presently heard
rapidly descending the stairs.   Mima was hastily
tying her bonnet to go out, when, bursting into the
kitchen, he declared that he had been robbed, his
money-drawer broken into, and some of his money
taken; and, heaping the most opprobrious epithets on
the whole family of the Higginses, he seized Letty by
the arm, and charged her with being the thief, declaring he would have her in jail before she was four-and-
twenty hours older.

Mrs. Higgins, casting a glance of fury upon poor
Letty, hurled back upon her lodger terms equally offen-
sive to those he had applied to her.

"She's stolen my money! she's broken in my money-
drawer!" said he, shaking Letty furiously.

Letty dropped down on her knees, and protested
her innocence, whilst Mima, looking nearly as pale, and

far more guilty than her sister, went out, glad to escape unobserved.

"Oh dear! dear! what will become of me!" said Letty. "I never touched the keys—I never opened the cupboard door!"

"You'll come to the gallows, as sure as you're born," said her mother, thinking perhaps to pacify her lodger by scolding the suspected culprit; "if you've done it, confess it at once! but as for me, I'm as honest a woman as any in Nottingham; I'd scorn to lay my finger on what was not my own!"

"Confess, you young baggage!" exclaimed Mr. Greaseley, "and give me back what you've taken, and then, for your mother's sake, who's a widow, I'll pass it over!"

"Confess!" screamed her mother, "or else I'll flog the life out of you!"

"Indeed! Indeed!" exclaimed poor Letty, "I've taken nothing—I've touched nothing! what can I confess? So as I love Mrs. Greaseley," said she, bursting into tears, "how could I steal anything!"

"Pshaw! pshaw!" exclaimed the lodger, in violent impatience.

"What can I say! what can I do!" returned she, in a passion of despair.

"Tell the truth!" thundered out the angry man.

"I do tell the truth—the honest, honest truth, and nobody will believe me; how was I likely to take the money? what should I do with it—I, that never go out anywhere?" reasoned poor Letty.

"I don't believe she has taken it—it's my certain belief, she's never touched the money," said Mrs. Higgins, changing again to her daughter's side.

"Thank you, dearest mother," exclaimed Letty, almost overcome by her mother's words, "thank you for that blessed belief—I never did take it!"

"You know where I keep my money?" said Mr. Greaseley, in a quieter, but not less angry voice.

Letty dared not answer that question by a denial—

she dared not confess the truth, and, bursting again into tears, exclaimed, with hysterical violence, "Indeed! indeed! I am not guilty!"

"I'll have a constable," said Mr. Greaseley, and, fetching his hat down stairs, went out.

No sooner had he crossed the threshold, than his wife called Letty up stairs. "Letty," said she, "I didn't think you would have done this!"

"I haven't done it," said Letty, bursting into tears; "I never touched the keys all the time!"

Mrs. Greaseley had been crying, but she looked now angry. "Do not tell stories, Letty," said she; "you have had the keys—you have been to the box— you know it! naughty girl! you know it!"

"Is there no possibility of God speaking from heaven for me!" exclaimed Letty, almost in despair. "Oh, I wish there was, and then you would know how innocent I am! I never opened the box—I never touched the keys all the time you were out—I tried to do all so right—I came and dusted everything every day—I was so happy in thinking I did well!— oh dear! dear! who can have done this?"

"Letty," said Mrs. Greaseley, grieved at what she thought her hardened wickedness, "how can you talk thus? I thought you were a good girl—I loved you, Letty—you have hurt me very much!" and the poor old woman burst into tears, whilst Letty threw herself on the ground in an agony, and wept too.

"It's no use all this crying," said Mrs. Greaseley, after a moment or too. "I've been deceived, sadly, sadly deceived! How naughty it is of you to have taken *his* money—Oh Letty! Letty!"

"I haven't, indeed I haven't," said the poor girl, in a low voice.

"You know you have," returned the other; "and, now to deny it so hardily, is more than I can bear. Confess, girl! now do, do confess, and I'll get you off some way or other. I haven't told him about you

M

taking the little housewife too—the pretty little brocade
housewife, that I set such store by."

"Is that gone too?" exclaimed Letty, in such un-
feigned astonishment as might have convinced any
one of her innocence; "the little housewife gone
too!"

"You know it is gone," returned Mrs. Greaseley,
provoked by what she thought her artfulness; "you
make me angry, Letty, by all this pretence of innocence: you know, you naughty girl, that you've
taken it; and I've a good mind to leave you to your
fate! Why will you try to deceive me?"

"It must be a dream!" said Letty; "it never can be
real—oh dear! oh dear! I wish I could wake!"

"Nonsense! nonsense!" said the old woman, "you do
really provoke me! Once more, Letty, before he comes
back, I pray you to confess the truth; it must and will
come out, if you don't; but if you confess and tell me
all, I'll get you off, one way or another; though I never
can love you again as I have done!"

"I think," said Letty, venturing to confess the only
truth which she could confess, and to hint a suspicion
which had dimly come into her own mind, "I think
Mima must have done it!"

"For shame! for shame! Letty," said the old woman,
"this is worse and worse! Would you make another,
and that your own sister guilty, and screen yourself?
I've done with you!" and, grieved at what she thought
Letty's hopeless depravity, she went into the chamber.
"It's not the value of the things," said she, again
coming back to the girl—"though I prized the housewife, and the money is a good deal—that grieves me
most, but that you have so deceived me—so as I
loved you, Letty!"

"You have been good to me, and I love you—oh,
I can't tell you how much," returned she, "and I
thought to please you so, while you were out!"

"What shall I say to you, Letty, dear?" said the good

old lodger; "how can I move you—how can I persuade you to confess—to me!—only to me!"

"Once, nay, twice," said Letty, in a trembling voice,
and dropping on her knees, "I did open the drawer,
and once I counted out the money"—Mrs. Greaseley
held up her hands, and almost held her breath—"but
that," continued Letty, "is very long since. I was
very wretched about it—I could not sleep at night;
but that was before I went to church. You told me,
that if I sinned, I must pray God to forgive me, and
he certainly would; I tried to pray for forgiveness, and
I thought I was forgiven. I love you—oh! how
much I love you!"

"You have been a very naughty girl!" interrupted
Mrs. Greaseley; "and now, where is the money?"

"I have confessed to you all," said Letty; "it is
very long since I opened the drawer, but money I
never took; while you were out, I never even touched
the keys."

Mrs. Greaseley shook her head, and said, "she was
very sorry, but she could not believe that."

"Then I will say nothing," returned poor Letty.
"if you will not believe me; and if you have ceased to
love me, I don't care what comes of me!"

The next morning, great was the crowd of turn-out
hands, and idle women and children, who thronged
about the police office door, to see Letty taken by her
accusers before the magistrates.

The case was stated. Mr. Greaseley told how
Letty was in habits of intimacy with his wife, and how
she knew all that the room contained. He described
his money as we know it was kept; it was, he said, his
savings for years; that he had, in coin of various sorts,
71l. 7s.; that among it were twenty sovereigns, and
seven half crowns. He kept a very exact account of
his money, he said, and never had missed any before:
there was no written paper in the bag, for he kept
the account in his head: the Sunday he was at home,

in his wife's absence, all was right: his habit was to
count his money every Sunday morning, when he
mostly added something to it; he never got confused
about the amount—it was impossible he could thus
have made a mistake: he didn't look at his money
during the week, but on the next Sunday morning
he found one sovereign and two half-crowns to be
missing. Letty Higgins made his fire for him, and
made his bed: he could not say but she was very
orderly and attentive; and he thought she liked his
wife; but he believed she had taken advantage of the
trust reposed in her; everything was left in her care;
she knew where everything was; and, with the excep-
tion of the two nights he had slept there, she had had
the whole week to pry into everything; he felt in his
own mind morally certain that she was guilty, and
he called upon the magistrate to punish her as such.

Mrs. Greaseley was then called forward. She
stated, in a low voice, and evidently with reluctance,
what she believed to be the truth. She was, she said,
very much attached to the girl, and had done all in
her power to make her more comfortable; her home
had been a very unhappy one, and she had taken her,
as it were, almost to live with her. Whilst Mrs.
Greaseley was thus speaking, poor Letty, who stood
near, in charge of a constable, darted forward, and
declared in the most passionate manner, that she could
keep still no longer; that all the world might think
her guilty, she did not mind, but that Mrs. Greaseley
should, was more than she could bear. "Gentlemen,"
exclaimed she, "I never could tell you how good, how
kind she has been! She cured me of my lameness; she
took me to church; she taught me my duty to God
and man; how, then, was I likely to rob her? Oh!
gentlemen, dont believe it! Indeed, indeed, I am innocent!" and then, covering her face with her hands,
she wept so bitterly, that there was scarcely a heart in
the room unmoved.

The magistrate said, he thought it probable that Mr. Greaseley was mistaken in the amount of his money; it was a bad way to keep money thus hoarded up; there was a bank for the savings of the poor, why did he not put it in there? He considered Mr. Greaseley extremely blameable.

This censure angered the old man exceedingly, and he was more vehement than ever for the committal of the supposed culprit.

Mrs. Greaseley was then asked what she imagined could have been the girl's motive for taking the money, seeing, as had already been stated, that she rarely went out, nor dressed at all extravagantly; in short, that there was no motive for her taking it. Mrs. Greaseley, in reply, said that she thought Letty naturally a good girl; the temptation she believed might be her desire to save money; she had worked at lace-work for these several years, and her mother had taken away her money, which was very hard, for she was not a woman in want. Letty, she said, had just began to put a little money in the Provident Society, and on some plea or other her mother even had got great part of this from her. Mrs. Higgins, who had come into the room during this part of the evidence, rushed forward at these words, and declared them "a base lie;" the Greaseleys, she said, wanted to take away her character; and, to prove how false were the words they spoke, she would appeal to Letty herself. Letty, however, at this moment had fainted; the utmost confusion prevailed, and Mrs. Higgins, continuing very violent, was removed from the room in charge of a constable.

When Letty was recovered, and order again restored, Mrs. Greaseley was again called upon, and she went on to say, that she was very sorry, but she was obliged in her own mind to believe Letty guilty, although the money had nowhere been found among her things; she intended, she said, no doubt to give it, by little

M 2

and little, to the collectors of the Provident Society, to make up the money that had been taken from her; she was a very good girl in the main, Mrs. Greaseley said, and she hoped the magistrates would have mercy upon her, for she was young, and, as they saw, little better than a cripple. She was then asked if she had ever missed anything before—if anything else was ever taken? No, said the good woman, casting a glance on Letty, which was intended to remind her of the little housewife; but Letty saw it not, for she was sitting in a state of almost stupor. No, no, she said, nothing else was missing; she believed Letty quite honest in the main. Was there nobody else about the place, she was then asked, who was likely to have taken the money. Mrs. Greaseley said, she did not suspect anybody; poor Letty was the only person who went into the room—she was the only person, she believed, who knew where the things were.

Letty was then asked if at any time she had been absent from the house long enough for any person to go into the rooms unknown to her; or if she had told anybody where Mr. Greaseley's money was? Letty looked at Mrs. Greaseley, and then at the magistrate, as if she did not comprehend the question; she did, however, but she dared not speak, in this presence, the suspicion for which Mrs. Greaseley had so severely reproved her; so, after the question had again been put to her, she said she didn't know; she couldn't remember; she had tried to be so careful; she meant to have given Mrs. Greaseley great satisfaction; Mrs. Greaseley had given her a gown just before; she meant to have pleased her if it had only been for that; she never thought this would have happened; somebody else had taken the money, but she didn't know who; she said she felt very ill, and wished she might have a glass of water. A glass of water was given her, which prevented her fainting a second time, and then the magistrate said nothing could be proved against her.

He recommended Mr. Greaseley to put his money in the bank, and Mrs. Greaseley, when she went out in future, to take her keys with her; and so the case was dismissed.

In less than a week the Greaseleys had taken other lodgings, and all the inhabitants of Bartram's Court and the adjoining streets looked upon poor Letty as a thief, although nothing had been proved against her; and everywhere Mrs. Higgins had to defend herself from the suspicion which the police report had made public. Letty's situation at home was miserable, as may well be imagined, although in the bottom of her heart her mother believed her innocent.

" I don't say that you took her money, Letty," said Mrs. Higgins, when she and her two daughters were together; "she's a good-for-nothing, lying woman to say that I took your money out of the Provident Society, and I don't believe the old fellow had lost any money at all; this, however, I know, that I have! I don't say who has taken it, but that one of you has, I am certain sure!" and then, looking first at one, and then at the other, and fixing a glance on Mima, which penetrated her to the very soul, she repeated, "one of you, I'm certain sure, has taken it, and you needn't think but I'll find it out one day or another."

CHAPTER XI.

HOW MONEY MAY BE SAVED, YET NOT BE SAFE; AND HOW BAD LEADS TO WORSE.

The day after the grand entertainment at Radford Folly was one of great excitement among the working classes. Active members of what was called the People's Association, deputed to arrange the business of the great strike, went from warehouse to warehouse, throughout the day, announcing the more general determinations, and inviting particular persons to join the sitting of the Association that night at their place of meeting. The well-established fact, too, of Weston's failure, and the terrible discovery that the deposits of the men had never been invested for them in the Savings Bank, created a general feeling of distrust, and, in the minds of the deceived individuals themselves, dismay and resentment amounting almost to fury.

Mrs. Jones rushed into the Fords' house that terrible Saturday, soon after Ford was gone out, the tatters of her dirty cap streaming behind her, and bringing with her into the house the smell, as it were, of poverty. " Here's a pretty piece of work!" said she, " I hope Ford's not been leaving money in Weston's hands for the Savings Bank!"

Mrs. Ford, thinking the unhappy woman must be drunk, asked her, nevertheless, in a hurried, anxious voice, "How? why? what did she mean?"

She then told how she had just come from the shop at the corner, where all were talking of this affair, and crying shame on Weston, so as never had been heard. She knew that Ford worked for Weston, and she feared he might have been putting money by—that was all.

Mrs. Ford put on her bonnet, and, filled with consternation, ran to the shop at the corner. They told her it was all too true. She then went forward to Weston's, where she thought her husband might yet be; the place was all shut up, but several men, who had been employed there, were standing about, all in a state of great excitement. They could not tell her, they said, where her husband was; they thought, perhaps at the Sir Isaac Newton, for many people were there this morning. Thither she went. Orator Timmins and about a dozen other men were in the upper room, where they held their meetings; they said Ford had not been there; they wanted to see him, and they wished she would send him.

Greater part of that morning she went from place to place, in hopes of finding him, for she was wretched to think what the state of his mind must be, and she wished at least to sympathize with, if not to comfort him; he was, however, nowhere to be found; all she could learn was from one of his fellow workmen, who said, that when Ford was assured of the unhappy fact at the Savings Bank itself, he had muttered something to himself, pulled his hat over his eyes, and set off—he supposed, home. She returned home, but he was not there; she then sent off John, and bade him go everywhere till he found his father. In the evening he returned, but had not found him. The wildest alarm took possession of his wife; where could he be? what had he done with himself? all kind of horrible apprehensions filled her mind. It was a wild stormy night; it thundered and lightened, and rained fiercely. Again she went into the town, passed Weston's, and to the Sir Isaac Newton; many people were in the streets, spite of the rain, for it was the market night, and she met many whom she knew; but from none of them and nowhere could she gain information of her husband. At length she met one who told her he had been met about eleven o'clock in the morning on the Gallows Hill—how dismal the name sounded!—that he was walking very fast; they thought he must be going to New Basford, or somewhere there. Poor Mrs. Ford turned her steps homeward, and, dispirited and forlorn, could not help weeping as she went.

Towards eleven o'clock Ford came home; he was dripping wet, and there was a wild, gloomy expression in his face, that appalled his wife. "Thank God!" exclaimed she, nevertheless, and, breaking up the fire, drew the armed chair towards it for him. "Where have you been all this time, John?" said she. He made her no answer, but sate looking into the fire.

"Oh, John, do speak, do speak," urged she, "I've been almost out of my senses all day for fear!"

"What were you afraid of?" said he, gloomily.

"Oh I don't know," replied she, "I had all kind of horrid fancies, and if I had known where you were, I would have followed you. Take off your things, pray do, or you'll get your death of cold!"

It made Ford angry to be urged by his wife to anything; he swore a terrible oath, and told her to hold her peace. "Oh my God!" exclaimed the poor man, at length, striking his hand upon his forehead, "only to think of it! all that money gone—so as I saved—so as I prided myself on it; I could almost have parted with my children rather than with it!"

"God forgive you!" said his wife; "God in Heaven forgive you! you shouldn't say so; we'll save yet—keep up your heart, John, and all may yet be well! Oh, you don't know what it is to have a wife and children that will work with you."

Ford burst into tears, and wept bitterly. "I felt almost mad," said he, at length getting calm, "when I heard it at first; as if I could have killed Weston, as if I could have set fire to his place, even if I must have died for it! I couldn't come home—I dared not trust myself at the Sir Isaac—so I set off, and walked straight and away, I cared not where, so that I only kept in motion; so I walked on and on till I found myself at Hucknal, and so back; and the worst I wish Weston is, that he may endure only what I have endured this day!"

The next morning, as Mrs. Ford expected, her husband said he felt ill, and stiff all over. He would not, however, stop in the house, but would go out; for it would do him good, he said. When he got into the market-place, a ranter preacher was just giving out the hymn to about a dozen people who stood round, a gathering cry to the sermon he was about to preach—

" Come, all ye valiant soldiers,
    The promised land's in view,
And Christ your conquering Captain,
    Will safely lead you through."

Ford stood and listened to the hymn, and listened also half through the sermon, although he attended neither to one nor the other. A large concourse of people collected there; and, towards the middle of the sermon, the young demagogue Curly Hearson threaded his way among them here and there, giving to particular persons an invitation to follow him immediately to a political meeting on the forest, at which Orator Timmins and a dozen or two others were going to speak It did not at that moment matter to Ford where he went, so, leaving the ranter preacher, he bent his steps toward the forest. It was to be a very large meeting; and from all streets, and lanes, and alleys, working men—not only lace-hands, but others of every other trade and calling, some in their Sunday things, and others not—were streaming towards the rendezvous.

The small extent of uncultivated common which lay at the north of the town—the small remains of the Nottingham side of the far-renowned forest of Sherwood—was the place chosen for many a congregation of the disaffected in those days; nay, indeed, for congregations of people on many and divers occasions. There it was that executions took place, till within a few years, and thence the highest point, used for that purpose, still went by the name of Gallows Hill. Cricketers met for their trials of skill on an artificial plain which was made for the purpose; boxers had their prize-fights there; there the races were held, and there the military were exercised; thieves and robbers, and even murderers, it was said, had taken refuge, and often lay concealed in the vast and ancient sand-caves with which the ground, even, it was believed, from the times of the Romans, was filled; asses—miserable, maimed, and ill-used creatures—and ponies and horses no better conditioned, with chained and clogged feet, fed there; poor children might always be seen at play there, and lean sallow-faced stockingers, and lace-hands, with their hands in their pockets, strolled about with a listless, melancholy gait; whilst here and there, in some retired hollow, you suddenly came upon a little rope-walk, where children sate all day turning large wheels, and ill-dressed men, with hemp wrapped round their bodies, paced backwards and forwards. It was a wild little region full of hollows, and overgrown with heath and gorse—a remnant of the old times; yet, nevertheless, to a mind which could see poetry in common things, and in the lowest estate of human life, not without deep interest.

Hither came, on this autumn Sunday, nearly two thousand men, all dissatisfied, and all ready hand and hand to promote, if not effect, a change in things. There were about a dozen speakers; there was no flourishing attempt at oratory, but a simple detail given first by one and then by another, of the want which was beginning to be felt so grindingly by all, stockingers and lace-hands, and all the poor alike. They told of children crying for food; of parents who would work but could not find work to do; of hard-hearted parish-officers who refused relief; of workhouses which were worse than prisons; of landlords who sold the bed from under the sick and the dying; and then stepped forward an old positive-looking man, known among them as Orator Haslam, and spoke of tax-collectors, and collectors of rates—of road-rates, and of poor-rates, and church-rates—which took the money which ought to buy the children's food. He spoke of bread which was taxed, and meat which was taxed, and of fuel which was taxed; and, the more he said, the more dark and determined grew the faces of all his listeners. After he had made an end, Ford stepped forward, and told of his savings, and how they had been snatched from him. He never thought how he said it, or of the number of auditors he had; but they all said he spoke like a parliament man, and should be one of their leaders; so they enrolled his name as one of the People's Association, cheered him vehemently

as a new and worthy brother, and then as vehemently
gave a universal groan for Weston.

When the excitement of the day was past, and Ford
returned home, he found himself more unwell than ever.
He said the ground was damp with the rain of the
day before, and his feet must have got wet with standing so long. From that day, for four weeks he was
confined to the house with a violent rheumatic fever.
His wife called in a doctor, and at the end of the
month the doctor sent in his bill. What an astounding
amount was that bill! Mrs. Ford remonstrated, and
the doctor told her that the poor had no business with
doctors. Why did not her husband go at once to the
infirmary or the dispensary? She heaved a deep sigh,
and, for the first time in her life, allowed herself to
think that they were poor. She took out every penny
she had in the Savings Bank, paid the bill, and told
her husband it was the last time they must ever send
for a doctor.

A new era had now commenced in the Fords' house.
For a month he had earned nothing: even if he had
been well, he could not have done so, on account of
the turn-out, which still continued, and which had now
occasioned unheard-of distress in the town. The very
masters were beginning to have compassion on the
sufferings of the people; and most lamentable were
daily, nay hourly accounts of the destitution which
prevailed. First, every article of luxury or pleasure
had been parted with; then, one by one, every piece
of clothing or furniture which by any possibility could
be spared, was either pawned or sold. The little
provision shops refused to supply anything farther on
trust; and every day, poor women and their children,
or whole families together, passed slowly through the
streets with famine-stricken countenances, and with
feeble husky voices, singing doleful ditties of poverty
and want. Bands of men perambulated the whole
country, begging for the relief of the destitute lace-

hands; whilst every door in the town was besieged by pale-faced boys and women, whose very attempts at respectability were far more touching than rags, offering small fancy articles for sale, and which, alas! they could seldom induce anybody to buy. Winter was approaching; provisions were rising in price; and people, whether rich or poor, looked on with anxious faces, saying they knew not what would be the end of it.

There are many people who are good-tempered and hopeful all day long, while everything goes smoothly with them, and as long as they are in good health; but, bring against them—nay, bring against anybody—a counter-current of adverse circumstances, and who has philosophy or nerve to keep a temper unruffled? The proverb says, " When Poverty comes in at the door, Love flies out of the window." That was not quite the case with the Fords; affection did not quite desert them, but the comfort and happiness of their fireside by this time was completely gone. Mrs. Ford often found it an inconvenient thing to have her husband always at home—the house was so small, they and their children were in one another's way so; it would be a deal better, she said, if they could part with their dining-table and one of their chests of drawers. She didn't like quite confessing even to herself, at first, that they only wanted the money. As soon as ever Mr. Bartram became urgent for his Michaelmas quarter's rent, she said, they must be sold.

The bonnet-making got worse and worse; in fact, it was worse than no business at all, for nobody, for long, had paid ready money, and now she could not get in one penny of her outstanding debts. She set John to write out her little bills, and then to go and try to collect the money; but some people, he found, had left their houses, or had been sold up for the rent the week before; others wondered how his mother could ever have the heart to send to them, declaring that if they came ever to be as rich as Jews she should never

again have a penny of their money; others were astonished at her impertinence, and told John he had
better not come near their houses again. In short, he
found that to collect debts was the most hopeless work
that was done.

The state of things in the town was as gloomy as
possible. The leaders of the turn-out still refused to
let any go in on the old terms, and, like stern inqui-
sitors, went from house to house to keep strict watch
that no work was done in private. The women, and
many of the men who were suffering most, became
violent against their own party. Half a loaf, they
said, was better than none; and, spite of all their
watchfulness, many a piece of lace was made and
worked in private, ready to be turned into money on
the first opportunity.

" I cannot bear this do-nothing state of things," said
Mrs. Ford; " we are all in a muddle down stairs together, and I'll get a piece of lace, as sure as I'm born,
and I and the girls will work it up stairs." Her husband said she had better not; and, while they were
talking, Mr. Bartram paid his long-apprehended visit.
He said it was now six weeks over the quarter, and he
would not wait any longer; he could get rents nowhere, and had at that very time executions in no less
than six different houses." Ford said it was a monstrous
cruel thing, seeing how badly off people were ; and so
said his wife, and that she thought, considering what
good tenants they had been, he ought to have patience
with them. Mr. Ford said he had been ill a long time;
that they had had a great doctor's bill to pay; he had
lost his savings by Weston's bankruptcy; and how this
turn-out had thrown them back sadly. Mr. Bartram
was tired of having the turn-out made a plea for non-
payment of rent : he said the turn-out was a great piece
of folly, and as people brewed so must they bake; he
must and would have his rent, and that was the long

and short of it. There was Mrs. Higgins, he said, at
the next house, just as much behind-hand as anybody.
Mrs. Higgins, he said, he used to think a very respectable woman, but he had now altered his mind; the
Joneses he should sell up stick and stone. He did not
say what he would do to the Fords; but the impression
of both husband and wife was, that if they did not pay
him within the three days which he granted them, he
would sell them up stick and stone also.

In the afternoon Mrs. Ford sold, for less than half
their original cost, her dining-table and chest of
drawers, and, after it was dark, went to an acquaintance about the lace-work; and next night, when it
was dark also, two pieces of lace, stamped in the pattern, and ready to work, were brought in, which she
carried up stairs, and the next day she and the two
girls sate down industriously to work.

Ford was still an invalid, much too unwell to go, as
formerly, among his acquaintance, either to the Sir
Isaac Newton or elsewhere; he, however, when the
noons were fine, put on his great-coat, and, with a
night-cap under his hat, might be seen slowly walking
about in the sunshine. One day, when he was thus
out, two persons, who paid occasional visits to prevent
work being done, came into the court; they walked
into Ford's house, and, seeing no one in the kitchen,
but hearing voices in the chamber, walked up stairs
without ceremony—for indeed ceremony was very
little used on such occasions. Mrs. Ford almost
screamed when, turning round at the sound of a man's
step on the stairs, which she at first imagined to be
her husband, she saw one whose terrible business she
instantly understood. It was no use attempting to
deny the fact of their being employed in the inter-
dicted work. The man nodded his head, and, though
he said nothing, looked full of black determination.

"What is one to do?" said Mrs. Ford, "to starve?

to have one's goods sold out of one's house? to go
begging? or, worse than that, to steal?"

The man said they were to bear!—that it was
shameful for people like them, who were well to do,
and had plenty to turn into money, to shrink and
grow impatient almost before suffering had touched
them! He said, let them look in at Jones's, at Griffiths's, at twenty houses even in that court, and see
what the people were suffering. Why, Joneses, he
said, had not a bed in the house, nor a blanket; and
Griffiths and his wife had pawned everything they
could part with: they had nothing to cover them at
night but an old rug—and there was she with a baby
only ten days old.

Mrs. Ford said she herself had sent the Griffithses
some things to make them comfortable, and had sent her
a jug of caudle; Mr. Griffiths was very poor, and she
was sorry for them; but, as things were going on, everybody would be poor; they were poor themselves, whatever he might think.

The man grew angry, swore a fierce oath, and said,
that when people were downright poor then they were
patient; but that such as the Fords were proud, and did
not know how to bear; such as they it was who made
a turn-out of no avail. Then, going down stairs again,
he marked a black cross on the door-post, and pro-
ceeded on his further visits. As soon as he was out
of the court Jane took soap and water and tried to
wash out the black mark, but it was indelible. Presently Ford was seen returning as fast as his weakness
would allow him: he had heard of the discovery which
had been made, and, troubled and angry, came back
to vent his feelings.

That night about fifty persons came to Ford's house,
to demand the lace: they said there were about a hundred pieces to be burnt that night; it was all done
secretly, for fear of the police, but that Ford, if he
liked, might come and see. John said he would, and

followed them. They went to the forest; and, as they had said, broken frames, and pieces of lace, some finished and some only in progress, were burnt in one of the largest and most retired caves, a little past midnight. It was a wild and terrible scene: the dark mouth of the cave, the sudden white blaze of the combustible material, and groups of desperate, hungry, and sickly-faced men that stood around, made altogether a picture worthy of Salvator Rosa.

The next Monday, after having stood out for five weeks, the men yielded; consenting to go in again on the very same terms for which they had turned out. Had they only persevered for that one day, the masters would have made them favourable proposals; but they heard that only too late, and the knowledge, when it came, only embittered their minds the more.

CHAPTER XII.

LITTLE COIN, MUCH CARE.

"Troubles always come in clusters," said Mrs. Jones to Mrs. Higgins, some months after this time. And here we may as well say that the family of the Joneses, after they had been sold up for rent, had taken refuge, themselves and their two or three miserable possessions, in the two rooms formerly occupied by the Greaseleys. How Mrs. Higgins managed to get her weekly payments might seem a little mystery; but, by dint of threatening and dunning, and keeping a sharp look-out whenever any money came into the house, she did contrive to keep tolerably straight. "Troubles never come singly," said she to her landlady; "only think now of the Fords, so high as they used to hold their heads, as if they thought nobody good enough to come near them! why, he gets drunk now every week, as sure as the week comes round; they've sold a power of furniture already, and she has offered all her blocks and her bonnet-making things for twenty shillings."

"Upon my word!" said Mrs. Higgins.

"They were talking of it in Harris's this morning," continued the lodger; "Harris said they owed him a good bit of money, and he would not trust them any more till they paid something in advance. He was very angry with them because they had been buying grocery goods from Tomlinson's—it was Tomlinson's sister who said she had all Mrs. Ford's blocks offered her—and now they've got the measles in the house!"

"And she'll be confined in a month or two," said Mrs. Higgins; "she may well try to raise a little money beforehand."

"I always knew no good would come of that bonnet-making and all that pride," observed Mrs. Jones; "and, with measles in the house, and another baby in her arms, this winter she'll have enough to do!"

"Thank Heaven," said poor Mrs. Ford, when the illness of the little Stephen was pronounced by the dispensary doctor to be measles, "the children have all had them excepting Stephen and the baby!"

Jane watched little Stephen night and day, and he soon recovered—not so the baby; it continued ill many weeks, and then appeared likely, if it escaped with life, to carry with it all its days a weakened constitution and diseased eyes. "It would be a great mercy," said Mrs. Jones, "if that little Ford died, for it's like enough to be a miserable object all its days." Mrs. Higgins said it was a judgment on them for holding their heads so high; and, as to this new baby of theirs, sure enough there never was its equal—all day and all night was it crying!" Mrs. Jones said that was true enough—she couldn't get a wink of sleep at night for it; there was Mrs. Ford walking up and down the chamber, and even Ford himself trying to pacify it, but to no purpose—it still cried on!

Mrs. Jones had said truly, that troubles always came in clusters—poor Mrs. Ford thought so also. The turn-out—the great doctor's bill—the bad state of the bonnet-making business—the loss of Ford's savings—the two pieces of lace which were burnt, and then had to be paid for—all gave a decided blow to the prosperity of the family. After this came the children's illness, and then the addition to the family; and even yet their troubles visibly were not at an end!

As Ford's health and strength returned he became, as it were, an altered man. The loss of his savings had made him reckless; there was a sense of coming poverty in his house, a discontent and anxiety in the countenance of his wife, that troubled and angered him; and, to avoid the lesser evils, he flew to greater ones. He went to the Sir Isaac Newton, or anywhere, rather than home; he made himself active in the People's Association, spoke at their meetings, drank at their clubs, and persuaded himself he was doing his duty as a suffering Englishman to his suffering fellows. Still, with all his efforts to put his troubles away from him, he was an unhappy man.

The sickly child and the young baby occupied a deal of time. "The Fords never had had," as Mrs. Jones said, "a baby that cried so much, slept so ill, and gave so much trouble, as this!" Rachel and John were the only two, beside the father, who had regular time for work. The mother, Jane, and even little Stephen, employed what moment of time they could spare in lace-work at home. "You should not keep that child at work all day long in that way," said one of the ladies of the Provident Society, who still now and then looked in on Mrs. Ford, although she had no money to put by. Jane stroked Stephen's soft brown hair, and said he never wanted to play. The mother said he was as meek and obedient as a girl, and liked to sit with them; and, besides this, they

wanted all the earnings they could get; they all
worked together, but still their united earnings were
hardly a pound a week.

Mrs. Ford thought it hard to manage when the
united earnings of the family were twenty shillings a
week: in a month's time after this, fifteen shillings
was the utmost they could raise amongst them.   Let
no one say the poor are bad managers!—but, with
bread at a high price, every potatoe to buy which they
consumed, rent, firing, and candle-light, how were eight
people to be fed and clothed out of fifteen shillings a
week? How could it be done, even if the father had
not spent a farthing in liquor?   Still, spite of this
pressure of poverty, the Fords were the most respectable family in the whole court: everybody looked up
to them, everybody thought that they might lend.
"Tell me not that they are poor," Mrs. Jones said to
her landlady; "Ford never gets drunk above twice in
a week, and they are all workers; they've still the
clock in the house, and the big chest of drawers, and
they still have best clothes to put on on a Sunday:
they won't lend—that's the thing!" Mrs. Higgins
said they had refused to lend her their mop last
Saturday, and she did not think she should ever ask
them again ; she liked neighbours to be neighbourly—
that she did!

Spite, however, of this heroic determination, Letty
came, in a day or two after, to the Fords, with a
broken basin in her hand, and asked them to lend her
mother some meal.

"What! is your mother at home to-day?" asked
Mrs. Ford.

Letty looked troubled, and coloured, and said her
mother did not always go out now on Wednesdays;
that they had had nothing but potatoes and salt for the
last three days; but that to-day her mother had a bit
of cold meat, and would make a hasty pudding, if
she could borrow a little meal.

There was something affecting in the melancholy
tone of Letty's voice; Mrs. Ford therefore said that,
although they had not much meal in the house, they
would lend her what they had.

" How ill that girl looks," said she, when Letty was
gone; "and she seems, too, to get crookeder every
day." Jane said that, since that affair of Mrs. Greaseley, Letty had never looked herself; she wondered if she
really were guilty. " Yes," Mrs. Ford said, " she feared
she was; she didn't think the Greaseleys would have
said so without cause; and other people must have
thought so too, for Mrs. Higgins had lost most of her
good places since then; and did not Jane remember
what was said about Mima? she was anything but a
respectable girl; still she could not help feeling sorry
for Letty." Jane said Letty looked as if she had not
enough to eat, and she did not believe she would ever
bring the meal back again. " I shall give over lend-
ing," said Mrs. Ford; "it was only last night Mrs.
Jones sent to borrow a candle." "And the day before," said Jane, " Mrs. Griffiths sent to borrow salt."
" God help us all!" said Mrs. Ford.

One day Ford came in and said the people were
determined on a strike for wages again, and that they
had all entered into a bond to subscribe a shilling a
week, as a fund to enable them to stand out.   His
wife held up her hands, and asked where the shilling
was to come from, unless he would save it out of the
money he spent in drink.   Nothing in the world is so
easy as to make a quarrel, especially between people
who have an under-current of dissatisfaction in their
minds, and who have ceased, from whatever cause it
may be, to be as open and confidential as formerly.
Ford and his wife quarrelled; the neighbours heard
the loud voices of contention: Mrs. Higgins and Mrs.
Jones stood with their ears in the chimney, to make
out, if they could, what it was all about; while the
wife at No. 8, who was a notorious scold, came to the

window, and listened, rubbing her hands, and saying
it was egg and milk to her to hear the Fords quarrel-
ling. The next day she went from house to house,
telling them that Ford had actually beaten his wife,
and they might just see if she wouldn't have a black
eye all the next week.

The spring came, the crocuses were in bloom; but
how different to that former spring of which we
wrote. A keen bleak east-wind cut them off as they
blew; children went to gather them, huddled up in
old shawls and cloaks, and, instead of running joyfully
about, stood shivering, with blue faces that spoke of
famine and discomfort.

There was something sorely ungenial in the season;
and when June came, and men spoke of the strike
which should take place, and held their meetings in
the hollows of the forest, or walked, in groups of ten
or twelve together, in the meadows, to talk over their
discontents, there came no cheering consoling influ-
ences from nature: the trees were hardly in leaf; the
same piercing winds swept over the face of the earth,
searing every green thing as if with hot iron. No
man returned to his house or his children with a
bunch of wild flowers in his hand; but, filled with the
spirit of evil augury, went to the beer-house or the
gin-shop, and took, as they said, a drop to put a bit of
life into them.

In the month of July the most fierce and burning
heat began—a stifling dry heat, as if from the mouth
of a furnace; and now and then came a rumour, as of
a baleful voice crying from a distance, of malignant
fever which had made its appearance here and there
in the town, the concomitant of want and discontent.
The medical men said the people must live better;
but how in the world were they to live better, when
the most sober and industrious among them could not
get bread enough to eat! The fever was found also
to be most fatal—to attack those soonest who had been

accustomed to a more respectable mode of life—whose minds were most depressed by their misfortunes.

"Griffiths is very ill," said Mr. Ford, one night; "I found him leaning against a lamp-post in the street, and complaining of racking pains all over him. I helped him home, and then ran for the dispensary doctor." Ford said he had been into Griffiths's bed-room, and that there was nothing but straw in it. Perhaps, said Mrs. Ford, her husband did not know that they themselves had but one feather-bed left, and that Mr. Bartram had been that day to say, in future he must have his rent weekly; the people at No. 8 had moonshined in the night, that is, had gone off without paying their rent; he was very angry, and threatened them; there was now three weeks due over the quarter; what was she to do? Ford could not tell. She went on, therefore, to say that Tomkinsons had refused to sell them anything more on trust; that she did not dare to go to Harris's even for a loaf of bread, unless their bill was paid—what was to be done? "What is to be done?" is the most aggravating ques-tion that can be asked of a man in embarrassed cir-cumstances. Sell something—pawn something—ask the parish for relief—turn highway thief—hang your-self!—these all may be resources; but they help very little, except to make matters worse. Ford got into a passion—it was the easiest way to answer his wife; and then, because she cried, and the baby cried, and their small room was hot and stifling, and the window when opened let in air from the court more stifling still, he went to the public-house, whose door and win-dow admitted fresher air, and added one more chalk against his name, to be wiped off on Saturday night when he got his wages.

CHAPTER XIII.

THE next day Ford came home from his work in the afternoon, and complained of pain in his head and back. " Griffiths is dead," said his wife, not thinking, till the words were out of her mouth, that perhaps her husband had the same fearful complaint. Two doctors came; they said they must have a ward in the hospital prepared, and that Ford must go there. There was nothing in this world which poor Ford dreaded like going to an hospital. He said he would not be removed; if he must die, he would die where he was. His wife also urged that he might stay, that she might wait upon him, for a yearning clinging affection filled her heart; she said that she had no fear, and would wait upon him herself. The medical men were not satisfied, and yet they acquiesced. Ford became dreadfully ill; the doctors looked on with anxious faces, the whole place was deluged with chloride of lime, and the children were forbidden to go into the chamber. In a day or two John showed symptoms of the same disease, and then the sickly child also. The utmost alarm prevailed throughout the court, and not a neighbour would come near them; nor even through the whole of the week was Mr. Bartram seen by one of his tenants, which was a happy circumstance for them all. Mrs. Ford and her two daughters waited on the sick day and night; the third day the father was pronounced somewhat better, but the sickly child died. There was hardly time for grief; the parish sent a coffin, and men to carry away the corpse, and Mrs. Ford, putting on her black gown and black bonnet, followed the poor child to the grave. When she returned it seemed to her that the lower room was hotter than usual, and she told Stephen to open the casement wider; the little fellow did so, but in doing

o

it unfortunately broke a pane of glass with the iron
fastening. In a rich man's house, in the house of a
person of easy circumstances, how easily is a favourite
child forgiven for breaking, by accident, a pane of glass!
In a poor man's house how different is the case—glass
broken is money completely lost; and what money
have the poor to lose? Full of grief as Mrs. Ford
was, and though she had seen one child laid in the
grave, she could not help being severely angry with
little Stephen, nay, even beating him for his fault.
"We are poorer by fourteen-pence," said she, "by
this blundering work of thine!"

Stephen went out into the court, and cried quietly
to himself; his mother's words, that they were poorer
by fourteen-pence through him, rung in his ears. He
had one little treasure in the world—a creature that
he petted and loved tenderly, a white rabbit, that
lived in the hole under the stairs;—if he were to sell
that, he thought, he could perhaps pay for the broken
pane. It required a long struggle with himself before
he could consent to make the sacrifice; and then,
determining to say nothing to any one in the house,
he went softly in, put his rabbit in a basket, his little
old cap on his head, and went out, intending to offer
it at all the houses in Castle-gate, one by one, till he
found a purchaser. Had the inhabitants of those larger
houses known that poor Stephen came from a dwelling
in which the terrible fever raged, he would have been
driven from every door; but there was something in
his meek soft countenance, his extreme youth, his
gentle troubled manner, offering for sale a creature
that in its gentleness resembled himself, that touched
the heart of the very first person to whom he offered
it. The purchaser, knowing how customary it was in
these times of distress for the poor to part with all
their little possessions, asked him no questions about
his home or his circumstances. Stephen said he
wanted fourteen-pence for his rabbit, and the kind-

hearted man gave him eighteen-pence, stroked his hair, smiled kindly on him, took the rabbit out of the basket, and told him then to make the best of his way home. The child would have liked to have kissed the creature before he parted with it, to have taken it to its new habitation, and have seen it eat once more, but there was no opportunity for that—the gentleman was gone—and little Stephen, feeling as if the sacrifice he had made was greater than he could bear, walked homeward, crying as he went. When he got home he could not help sobbing and crying bitterly; but he would not tell any one what he had done, or how he had got the eighteen-pence which he gave his mother for the broken pane. The next morning he sate with his head on the table, as if he were sleepy. "What's amiss, dear?" asked Jane. He said his head was bad; he thought it was with crying so last night. "Oh, gracious Heaven!" exclaimed his sister, bursting into tears, "he's got the fever!" Rachel and she brought down a mattress, and made him a bed in the kitchen; and when the doctor came, without feeling his pulse, or asking any questions, he ordered him a dose of the same medicine which the dead child had taken, and part of which still remained. John had a bed in the father's room; and Mrs. Ford, with the baby in her arms, attended on them, whilst Jane devoted herself to this most beloved child, and Rachel went and came and did errands for all. Poor Mrs. Ford! how it troubled her to think of having beaten little Stephen; and now (for the rabbit was found to be missing) she knew how he had gained the eighteen-pence. "Please God to restore him from his sick-bed," said she to herself, "I'll make him amends, let us be poor as we may!"

"Will not Jane come and see me?" asked John from his mother, as she gave him his medicine, on the fourth night of his illness, "I do so want to see her!" "Poor Stephen's very badly down stairs," said she, "but I'm sure she'll come!" "Can't you stay a bit," said he, "as, an hour afterwards, Jane came to his bedside, and seemed impatient to get away again. "I can't, indeed I can't, John," said she, "there's nobody down stairs with Stephen." He let go the hand which he had been holding, and, ill and out of spirits as he was, lay and cried to himself; and then the fever became raging, and through the whole of the night he was delirious. The doctors gave hope for Ford, but said they could give none either for John or Stephen.

"I'm sure Stephen's not worse," said Jane, "he opens his eyes; he knows me yet when I speak! oh, it is so wrong of them to say he is worse!"

A nurse from the infirmary was sent to them, for the doctors said they would all be ill with want of rest and with fatigue, if with nothing else.

"Oh Lord!" exclaimed the nurse, looking at Stephen.

"He's better," said Jane, "a deal better; now, see if he do not know me! Stephen, dear!" said she, stooping down to him, "look at me, dear—don't you know me?" repeated she, in a voice that faltered as she spoke. Stephen opened his eyes, looked at her, and then faintly smiled.

"Oh the dear, dear child!" said Jane; "I never loved any human creature as I love him;" and then, stooping down to his mattress, she smoothed the hair which lay disordered on his pillow, and prayed in her heart, that in whatever way it might be the will of Heaven to afflict them, that Stephen might still be spared." She would not go to bed that night, although both her mother and the old nurse urged it; she sate by his side, moistened his lips, and bathed his forehead. In the very early morning, while she was doing thus, he opened his eyes suddenly, and looked wildly about him. "It's a spasm, maybe," said the old woman, whom Jane summoned to her side, "I think, poor dear, he won't be long." "Oh don't say so, don't say so!"

exclaimed she. A sound was heard from his lips as if he would speak. " What is it, dearest ?" asked Jane, and bent her ear towards him. He half raised himself in the bed, as if suffering from internal pain; then, convulsively grasping the hand of his sister, stretched himself out, and lay still. Jane did not stir till the little hand relaxed its grasp, and then looking into his face, she perceived that an awful change—a change not to be misunderstood—had come over it—the beloved one was dead. How unquestionable was the fact; yet how long and obstinately did the heart refuse to believe it. " Can nothing be done ?" she asked, almost frantically. She proposed a warm bath—she proposed to fetch the doctor, but the old woman said it was no use, closed the eyes, and tied up the chin, and in the kindest way she knew, tried to comfort the poor girl.

It never occurred to Jane to go up stairs and call her mother; but, throwing herself at the foot of the bed, she lay there and wept bitterly; while the old woman, to whom death was a familiar thing, stood at the open door, and smoked a pipe. John and the father both slept a little. this night, and the mother, who dropped asleep also in the chair where she sate, did not know what had happened till daylight.

The next morning Jane sat down to work, to quill narrow net with extraordinary care on one of Stephen's nightgowns. All the time she worked she kept crying; but she said not a word, either to her mother or sister, of what she was doing. Both John and the father asked how Stephen was; and the mother, who stood by, fearing to confess the truth to them in their weak state, said that Stephen, poor dear child, was gone to sleep. Before long, Jane had finished her work—a shroud for the dead; the parish coffin was brought; there was no time to wait, they said; he must be buried immediately, because, as the weather was so hot, there was great danger of infection. Jane's tears ran down

o 2

anew; she and her mother, without speaking a word to each other, clothed him in his last apparel: they cut off several locks of his beautiful hair, and then, with many many tears, saw the coffin lid closed down upon him. Jane said that their mother had better not go with him to the grave, because the father and John would miss her; and that she and Rachel would go. There was no time to prepare mourning; nor, so great was the fear of infection, would any neighbour have lent any, had they asked. The two girls, therefore, put on what of black they had, and, with the deepest, truest mourning in their hearts, followed the beloved one to the grave.

Whilst this sorrow was yet freshest in their hearts, a new sorrow—a sorrow more severe than all the former ones—fell on the whole family: the mother herself became ill. Poor Ford got up from his sick-bed to wait upon his wife. "Please God to take all that ever I possess, children, home, and all," said he, in the anguish of his soul, "but leave me her!"

The news that Mrs. Ford was ill, and likely to die, rang through the whole of Bartram's Court like a knell. Poor Letty came in in the morning—she was the first neighbour who had come near them—and said, that if they would please to let her, she would take the baby home with her, and nurse it. She said the Jonesses were gone—they had gone three days before—that nobody would let her mother go to their houses now a-washing, because of the fever; and that she was that day gone to Kimberly—she did not know for what; she was not at all afraid of the fever herself, and would therefore take charge of the baby. "Oh, I've been so sorry for you all," said the poor girl; "I've come and come to the window to peep in, to see how Stephen was; I was so fond of Stephen, you can't think!" and then she began to cry almost as bitterly as the girls themselves. "Do let me have charge of the baby," said she, taking it out of Rachel's arms.

The girls said she should, and that they were very much obliged to her. The doctors refused to give a decided opinion about Mrs. Ford; and the old woman sprinkled about the chloride of lime more strenuously than ever. At night, when Mrs. Higgins returned, she seemed surprised, but not displeased, to find the baby in Letty's care; and, hearing that Mrs Ford was no better, went in herself to ask further after her—the first time she had been in the house for months. When people are in great sorrow or perplexity of mind, they are astonished at nothing; it might therefore have been the most natural thing in the world for Mrs. Higgins to be a good neighbour, from the manner in which the girls received her offers of assistance. Jane gave her a bundle of linen to wash, the moment she suggested such a thing; and Rachel said, " Oh, if she would but sit up all night with her mother, as she proposed, how kind it would be !"

The second day Mrs. Ford was delirious; her husband forgot that he had been ill; John, that he was yet so; and even Jane forgot that Stephen was dead, so overwhelming was their anxiety for her; the third day she fell into the stupor which, most probably, preceded death. The doctors did not talk of danger; neither did the old nurse; and, to the very last, all the poor Fords had hope.

Mrs. Higgins was supporting her head when she died. She seemed uneasy for some time before this happened, as if something were on her mind, but whatever it might be, she died with it unexpressed. Her husband was too weak in mind and in body to do anything but sit beside her and weep ; saying, every now and then, she would be better—he was sure she would! she was such a strong and healthy woman, there could really be no doubt about her! Poor man! he was deceiving himself with that false hope at the very moment when she died.

When, indeed, this astounding and terrible fact no
longer admitted of doubt, who can describe the agony
of the bereaved family! There was now nothing left
to fear beyond this, certainly; but after this there was
nothing left, as it seemed, worth living for. They gave
way to the natural impulse of grief, and sate down and
wept as if their hearts would dissolve into tears. Jane,
poor girl, thought neither about shroud nor cap for the
dead; the old woman and Mrs. Higgins did all that
was needful; nor was it till the very moment when the
coffin came, that any consciousness of the reality of
things fell again upon her heart. She saw then that
Rachel had prepared some little mourning, and that
one or two neighbours, filled with sympathy for the
bereaved family, and full of respect for the dead, stood
about the door, prepared to accompany her to the
grave. Jane hastily threw on her bonnet and shawl,
and walked, the saddest, truest mourner, behind the
coffin.

CHAPTER XIV.

AN EXODUS.

A weary twelvemonth went on. Time is a wonderful
alleviator of grief; but time also often only makes
more apparent the true cause we have for grief. So
it was in the family of the Fords. The father, stricken
both in body and mind by his illness, but still more by
the loss of his wife, felt as if the charm and value of
existence were gone—as if, stripped and alone as he
was, he had no power, no will even, to strive against
the current of evil fortune which had set in against
him. He was like one who, seeing a raging fire in his
possessions, should fold his hands together, in the stupor of despair, and make no effort to save ought—as
one in a vessel driven before the tempest, who should

neither shift helm, nor take in sail, saying, "What matters it? come what will, I am a ruined man!"

For many weeks after his wife's death, Ford might
be seen, on a Sunday, or on days when he did not work,
strolling through the meadows, pale and feeble, the
picture of hopeless grief. His associates told him this
would never do; that he must come once more among
them; must go once more with them to the public
house, and to their political clubs and meetings. Here,
to a certain degree, he found forgetfulness of his trouble; and with forgetfulness came recklessness, from
which his children could not redeem him.

As week after week, and month after month, went
on, poverty made itself more and more evident; now
a table—now a bed—and, at last, the clock—the idol of
poor Mrs. Ford's household worship—was sold. The
three elder children worked hard, but their earnings
were as nothing; they strove hard, too, to keep together their household possessions, but their efforts were
to no purpose.

The father said that they were too young to manage
—that things did'nt go on in this way in the mother's
life-time. Mrs. Higgins said the same; she would now
and then come in of an evening when Ford chanced to
be at home, and talk of prudence and economy, and
all household virtues, as if they were centred in her
person; she sate and nursed the baby, and kissed it,
and gave it sugar-plums, calling it the sweetest child
that ever lived; and declaring that she loved it as if it
were her own. The girls began to think her a good
neighbour; the father had thought her so long.

One day she came in, and said she was going to
leave her house; that she was going into lodgings, but
had been disappointed of those she wished to take,
and, as she must leave that day, was compelled to ask,
as a great favour, that she might put a few things into
the Fords' garret, which, since the mother's death, they

had not used. The girls thought there could be no
harm in that, and consented; when the father came
home in the evening, she said she had just been thinking, that perhaps they would let her lodge there altogether: Mima worked out all day, and Letty could
work with them at home, and she herself would take
a general oversight of things. The garret, she said,
would be quite enough for her and Mima; and Letty
could have a bed in the room in which the two girls
and the baby slept. Ford agreed at once; and Mrs.
Higgins, who had all the time had an eye to this
arrangement, settled herself down at once as mistress
of the whole place, taking care, however, to do nothing
which should give Ford himself cause of displeasure.

One day, a month or so after Mrs. Higgins had
thus established herself, John told his sister Jane that
he wanted her to walk out with him, as he had something very particular to say to her. "Jane," said he,
after they had walked some time in silence, "I am
going to leave you."

"To leave us!" repeated she.

"I can't bear it any longer," said he; "I cannot
stand by, and see that woman taking mother's place; I
shall quarrel with her—I shall quarrel with father, if I
stay. You don't know what's coming, Jane."

"You think father will marry Mrs. Higgins," returned
she, speaking out a suspicion which had been dim in
her own mind.

"I'm sure of it," he replied; "but it's what I'll never
stay to see. I should knock her down the day father
made her his wife. Only think of our mother," said
he; "how nice she looked; how pleasant and kind she
was; how cheerful and respectable she made our home.
There are not many women in this world, Jane, like
what our mother was! You are a deal like her in person, Jane; never forget her, and try to be like her in
heart also; keep her memory fresh in your soul, for my

sake, Jane—do!" said he, weeping. They both wept,
and turned into a lonely part of the meadows, that they
might talk and weep, unseen by any.

"And where are you going, and when?" asked she,
at length.

"I am going this very day," said he; "I shall say
good-bye to nobody but you. I have saved a little
money, and a few of my own things I have sold to
raise a little more; my bundle is already at the turn-
pike; and at eight o'clock I shall go there and take the
coach to Leicester; I know a young man there who
will help me to employment of one kind or another."

"Oh don't go," said his sister; "what will become
of us when you are gone?"

"Far better without than with me," returned he;
"father and I have parted company; I see plain enough
which way he is going, and that is not my way. If I
were to stop, I should be like a fire-brand in the house.
I shall write to you sometimes; and of this be quite
sure, that come what may, I shall never forget you—
that I shall never cease to love you!"

Jane was too much overcome by her feelings to
speak; and, after a few moments, her brother resumed:
"I went to mother's grave last night; I had some
trouble to make out justly where it was, but I have
found it: it's the seventh grave from the right hand
corner as you go in. Little Stephen's is just beside it.
Go there sometimes; it will do you good. I had more
on my mind last night than I could well bear; but,
after I had sate there maybe an hour, and thought over
my plans, I felt stronger and calmer, and a better man
than I had done for months. It seemed to me as if my
mother's spirit came and comforted me."

"Oh, brother," said Jane, "I have not been to you
what I ought to have been. I have never loved you
enough: stay with us, do stay, and I'll be so different!"

"I should kill that woman, or do some mischief,"
said he, "if I staid! It has made me almost mad

when I have thought of her sleeping on mother's pillow! I cannot stay, Jane. It is my good angel that has put it in my mind to go! And now, good bye!" said he; " the clock has just struck seven—good bye! and may God in heaven bless you!" added he, kissing her, and with his eyes full of tears. "Give my love to Rachel, and think of me sometimes!"

"I'll go with you," said she, "to the turnpike-gate, to see you off. I almost think you are right, if you can get employment elsewhere, to go; and if father really marries her, I'll follow your example too!— Only to think! and what's to become of that poor baby!" And Jane, overcome by her feelings, stopped short to weep again.

At eight o'clock the mail passed through the turnpike-gate, and John mounted with his bundle, waving, to the very last turn of the road, a farewell to his sister.

Ford felt the absence of his son a relief, and Mrs. Higgins hardly concealed her triumph.

John was right: in less than twelve months after his wife's death, Ford made Mrs. Higgins his second wife.

"Jane says she'll go out to service," said the new Mrs. Ford to her husband, about a week after her marriage; "and let her go; she behaves shameful to me! Rachel I can do very well with: she and Mima agree like sisters; but Jane has the spirit of a dragon!"

"I cannot bear to see that woman wearing mother's clothes," said Jane to her father; "I didn't think it would have come to this—that poor mother would so soon have been forgotten."

Ford looked abashed and troubled, and did not attempt one word in his own justification. The truth was, he knew that he had taken a wrong step.

"There are too many of us already in the house," continued his daughter. "I cannot earn my own bread at the lace-work; and why should I starve

here, or be a burden to anybody? If you are happy,
father, with this new wife, all well and good—but I
must go!"

Ford said there could be no harm in her going to
service; and that she should have part of her mother's
clothes, and Rachel the rest; and that the next day
they should be divided. Poor Ford, in intending this,
however, had reckoned without his host. His new
wife had got possession, and would give up nothing;
the keys that locked up the former Mrs. Ford's wardrobe were in the bottom of her large pocket, and no
power on earth, she declared, should get them from
her: as for Jane, she said, she only wished her to go
out of the house, and never darken the door more.
The father was appealed to by both daughters; and
the new wife defied them all three. Bartram's Court,
therefore, the next morning had the pleasure of talking over how Ford had actually beaten his wife, and
how Jane had been turned out of doors by her new
stepmother.

"They are all bad together," said Jane, in the
warmth of her feelings, talking to the widow Griffiths,
with whom she had taken refuge that night; "and it
makes my heart ache to think of Rachel, who is just
the girl to be ruined by one like Mima! The only one
of the Higginses that has a grain of goodness in her
is that poor Letty; and she takes care of the baby just
as if it were her own sister. I should be more miserable than ever, were she not there to look after it!"

The widow Griffiths went out to inquire in the
neighbourhood if anybody wanted a good servant;
while Jane, in the absence of her stepmother, went
home to pack up her clothes and give a little parting
advice to her sister.

"I'm more cunning," said Rachel, in reply to her
sister's warning, "than you think me. I'm not going
to quarrel with her—that's all; but I hate her just as
much as you do! Nor need you be afraid of Mima

P

corrupting me—I can take care of myself, never fear!
I shall come and see you sometimes, let you be where
you will; and you need not fear leaving little Sally—
Letty is so good to her you can't think: she was up with
her almost all last night, because she cried so for you!"

" Poor thing!" said Jane, pausing in the midst of
her small packing, " I must see her sometimes; but I
sha'n't often come here, I promise you!"

When Jane, assisted by her sister, carried down
stairs the papered trunk, bandbox, and bundle, that contained all her worldly effects, she found Letty there,
with little Sally asleep on her lap.

" Good bye, Letty," said she, after she had kissed
her little sleeping sister; " I shall be at Mrs. Griffiths'
till I get a place: come and see me sometimes—and,
oh Letty, you'll take care of Sally—I'm sure you will!
and, you may depend upon it, there'll come a blessing
to you for it—I'm sure of it," said she.

" Jane," said Letty, after a pause, "just let me ask
one thing from you before you go, and which I've
often and often wanted to ask—for I love you, Jane;
indeed, indeed I do! Do you really and truly think
that I robbed Mr. Greaseley?"

" No," said Jane; "someway or other I don't think
you did."

" No, indeed I did not," said the poor girl, her lips
quivering with emotion; "and I love you better than
ever for saying so; and all that ever I can do to please
you I will! Now, just listen one moment longer, Jane,
said she: " Mrs. Greaseley gave me a printed gown
for myself. I haven't many nice things, you know;
and I was so proud and pleased to think how nice I
should look in this!—but, oh dear, I never could make
it up after what happened: to think only that she
believed me a thief! No, Jane, I put the gown by;
for I felt as if I should lose my senses when I thought
of it; and how could I help thinking of it when I saw
the gown? I shall never wear it myself; but I'll tell

you what I will do—I'll save it for little Sally. I
shall make Sally love me very much—I hope nobody
will tell her that people believe me a thief!" At the
bare idea of this Letty burst into tears. Jane wept
too, and then gave Letty a kiss; and then, opening
her bonnet-box, took out a pretty blue-and-white silk
handkerchief, which on Sundays she wore round her
neck.

" Take this as a keepsake, Letty," she said, "from
me—I haven't worn it many times; but perhaps you
will not like it the worse for that."

Letty's tears flowed faster than ever; and, assuring
her again and again that she would take good care of
little Sally, she watched her across the court with a
heart swelling with gratitude and love.

The widow Griffiths told Jane that they wanted a
servant at the Ruben's Head; that they would give
her four pounds a-year wages, and, if she liked, she
might go there that very night. Jane was not quite
satisfied, but the widow said so much in praise of the
mistress of the house, that she consented; accordingly,
that same evening the papered trunk, the bandbox,
and bundle were carried by the widow's son Mark
out of the court, and Jane Ford begun her days of
servitude.

CHAPTER XV:

A CONFLAGRATION, AND ONLY ONE RAY AT SUNSET

ONE of the most painful discoveries that Ford made in
his new wife was that she drank. That a man should
drink—even that he should get drunk seven nights
in the week—he fancied hardly more than natural;
but for a woman to do so only occasionally filled him
with disgust and indignation. But when, beyond this,
Ford saw his new wife drunk whilst wearing his old
wife's clothes, the measure of his growing aversion to

her, and dissatisfaction with himself, was full. He had
deceived himself with the idea that Mrs. Higgins was
a tidy managing woman, who would keep things in
order, and bring back to his house something of its
former comfort, if not prosperity. He very soon came,
therefore, to think his children were right, and to wish
that he, like them, could flee from her altogether. He
did, however, towards this as much as lay in his
power—he was very little at home. If he were disappointed in his marriage, so likewise did she declare
herself to be; they lived literally, as the neighbours
said, like cat and dog; and Mr. Bartram declared that,
even if they paid their rent as punctually as formerly,
he would turn them out of his house—that he would—
were it only to be rid of such disreputable people. He
threatened; but, as long as there was furniture in the
house, he did no more than threaten; at length, however, seeing that first one thing went and then another,
and that before long the whole place would be as
stripped and bare as No. 6, when Mrs. Higgins first
entered it, whilst she had ceased to be that hard-work-
ing regular woman that she then was, he sent an execution into the house for the rent which was then due,
and cleared the greater part of the remaining furniture away.

Since Mrs. Higgins's marriage, she had troubled herself very little about going out washing; her best
places, from a variety of causes, she had long lost; she
seemed to think her husband ought to earn enough for
her maintenance, and what more was needed she
made out by selling and pawning. She had many
acquaintance up and down in the neighbourhood, too,
of a very doubtful character; among them was that
Mrs. Ward with whom she went, as our readers may
remember, to the gardens of Radford Folly. Sal Ward,
as she was generally called, was a large fat and dirty
woman, whose husband, known by the name of Black-
ball, dealt in dogs, which he stole more frequently

than bought: rags also they dealt in, and bones. Ford had a particular dislike both to this woman and her husband, and they were a perpetual source of discord between him and his wife. Another of her associates was her former lodger, Mrs. Jones, who, with her two wretched children, and drunken profligate husband, seemed sunk to the lowest pitch of poverty and degradation. Jones had been imprisoned for poaching, and taken up on suspicion of theft: they were a ragged, half-starved, dirty, and low-lived family; but, nevertheless, favourites of the new Mrs. Ford. Sal Ward and Bet Jones were notorious women through the whole neighbourhood; and, fallen in character, and fallen in self-esteem as poor Ford was, nothing aggravated him so much as to see these women at his house.

In this wretched home of poverty, discomfort, and disunion there still remained, however, one little glimmer of light, one little glimmer of love and joy—and that was poor Letty, in whose heart lay a deep fountain of affection and truth. Little Sally could not justly be said to grow and prosper, for she looked like what she was—the stunted child of poverty; but in Letty's eyes she was as beautiful as an angel. She ate of her morsel, drunk of her cup, and at night slept in her bosom, and was to her more than all the world beside.

There now approached in Nottingham a time of great political excitement. The people expected that the passing of the Reform Bill would bring about the most extraordinary change—would certainly restore the times of the old prosperity. An era was at hand, said Orator Timmins, which would be remembered in the annals of Europe. " Men of Nottingham," he said, " the eyes of the world are upon you; but you must be up, like men, ready to act—ready to strike the blow— to do the deed; always remembering the words of the dying hero, that ' England expects every man to do his duty!'" People did not exactly know what he meant

by all this and a great deal more; but they shouted
hurrah! and hear, hear! and then joined their hands in
token of a great brotherhood., Ford, who was there
when these words were spoken, and who was half-
drunk, shouted hurrah! with the loudest, and joined
his hand to theirs. Orator Timmins went on to say,
that they and their children should eat beef—the best
that was fed in the meadows of the Trent—at two-pence
a pound; and drink ale, the best that was brewed in
Nottingham, at two-pence a quart; and that their wives
should wear silks and satins, and sit with their feet on
footstools, like the finest ladies in the land; only they
must remember, that England expected every man and
every woman also to do their duty. "Hurrah! bravo,
bravo!" shouted women's voices behind; and Ford,
looking round, saw his wife, with her stiff crimped cap
and hard features, linked arm in arm with Sal Ward
and Bet Jones. He felt disgusted and offended; and
went, therefore, and drank another quart of ale, and,
the rest of the evening, roared and shouted with the
wildest of them, nor thought any more of his wife or
her associates.

The next Saturday night, the people were ready, as
their orator said, "to do their duty;" meetings were
held at all their places of rendezvous; the time was at
hand for action—the measure, their leaders said, for
which they were striving, was impeded in its progress
by the people in power—by people who had money
in their hands. All manufacturers, all people of landed
property, were therefore their enemies; and now they
must hold themselves in readiness to dare and to do!

It was a wild, stormy Sunday in October. Ford and
his wife, as usual, had quarrelled; and, with a feeling of
aversion towards his home, he joined the hundreds
who, after having awaited the arrival of the mail, and
received with groans, and every token of abhorrence,
the news that the bill was thrown out of the House of
Lords, were now bending their steps towards the

forest, where a very great meeting was summoned.
There was something wild and troubled in the very
air; the wind went soughing and sobbing through the
almost leafless trees, and brushing its viewless wings
with melancholy sighings over the pale discoloured
heath-flowers which had so lately been one blush of
crimson. Ford was disheartened, and yet desperate.
It seemed to him as if his life lay before him cheerless
as the barren waste, over which the winds of autumn
were then passing.   There seemed nothing left to
cheer—no one flower in the desert path of his life; he
seemed to have forgotten his children—to have neither
joy nor hope left. With a hundred such men as he,
Orator Timmins might have burnt all Nottingham.

That night they paraded the streets of the town,
broke many windows, uttered desperate threats, and cast
a panic into all hearts.

"Arms! arms! give us arms!" said Ford, half-drunk,
the next day; "give us arms, and we will do great
deeds!" Their leaders said, they must arm themselves
as best they could—that sticks, staves, crowbars, and
iron palisades, were better in the hands of brave men
struggling for their rights, than guns and swords in the
hands of hirelings! Whoever has wrongs to avenge,
said they, now is the time! Vengeance never lacks
its weapons!

"Would that Weston had a factory here!" said Ford;
"for then we would burn it to the very ground!"

"Burn!" re-echoed a hundred terrible voices; and
they moved off for vengeance, gathering strength as
they went, like the mountain snow-ball.

Here and there, therefore, through that day, the
smoke of fires were seen ascending; and the people of
the town, terrified at this unexpected outbreak, knew
not what to do. Jones, who had been imprisoned for
poaching by the master of Colwick Hall—a fine old
mansion, about two miles from the town, and standing

in the midst of old woods near the Trent—now gave
the word, " To Colwick! let us go to Colwick!"

How often had poor Ford walked, on a Sunday
evening, with his first wife, through these pleasant
woods, and down to this stately old house! but he did
not think of that, as, roaring and shouting forth their
hatred and their threats of vengeance, the infuriated
thousands rushed along the wood-paths, waving their
torches under tall, leafless trees, and among garden
evergreens, like so many demons. The iron palisades
of_the garden were torn up for weapons; and these
being of great length, and pointed like spears, were
most formidable. The servants abandoned the house
in terror, carrying with them the lady of the mansion,
who was ill, on a bed, and concealing her in the shrub-
bery till a boat could be obtained to convey her across
the river; and the mob, having applied fire with sufficient assiduity, as was believed, to consume the whole
pile, without even stopping for plunder, rushed back
again to the town.

Jane Ford stood at the upper windows of the Ruben's
Head, as one detachment of the rioters marched up
that street, the better to make their way to the market-
place. They carried torches in their hands, which, in
the darkness of the night, made their persons easily
recognisable.

" Gracious Heavens!" exclaimed Jane, starting back,
for she distinguished her father. She did not tell the
girl who was with her what she had seen; but, putting
her apron to her eyes, cried silently to herself.

" Come Sal! come Bet?" said a loud woman's voice
under the window, " I wouldn't give a pin if I wern't
in the midst of it!" Jane knew the voice only too well,
without looking out; it was that of her stepmother.
" And those women are going, too!" said the girl;
" what dreadful creatures they are—without bonnets,
and looking just as if they were tipsy!"

Before long, a man came rushing into the Ruben's Head, saying that the castle was on fire. It was a pitch-black night, and the rain poured down in torrents, but the flames burst out from window after window, rushing along the front of the building like immense tongues of fire. A roar, as of the sea lashed by the tempest, came downward to the town—not only from the consuming element, but from the infuriated thousands who were doing their work of ruin. Before long, the immense roof of the building fell in, deadening the fire for a moment, and then feeding it into tenfold strength; whilst burning pieces of wood, and whole columns of raging sparks, were carried upward, as from the mouth of a volcano, and scattered to a vast distance. All below, around, and above, appeared solid darkness; and the castle itself, with its innumerable windows, seemed like one immense furnace, lighting up the town and the surrounding country with a red and horrible brightness.

Jane stood at a distance, and looked on in terror, thinking that, probably, some one of those black figures, that seemed to be passing, as it were, in the very midst of the fire, like demons in the regions of burning, was her father; and that probably, also, in some of those yelling cries, which were sent forth as in the very rapture of devastation, was mingled the harsh, loud voice of her stepmother.

There was but little sleep in Nottingham that night; and, hour after hour, till it was again broad daylight, bands of men marched through the streets armed with their wild and terrible weapons, with torches in their hands, singing songs of vengeance and defiance.

The next day, the yeomanry cavalry were called up, and orders given to the regular troops stationed in the town barracks, to disperse the people, and to fire upon them if need were; when, after making a brave show of defiance and resolution, for a few minutes, they dispersed, and then fled like fallen leaves before a sudden gust of wind; proving, as, indeed, has been proved so often, how vain is the struggle of the people, even for their best rights, when their only measures are violence and physical force. Then, too, was heard an outcry for children who were missing, and who were supposed to be buried among the burning ruins of the castle. Search was made; and now one, and now another was found; and terrible and heart-rending was it to see parents and friends recognising or rejecting the scorched and defaced corpse as the missing one.

"No, no, this is not my Johnny!" said one poor woman, as the mangled remains of a child were dragged from under a mass of stone; "my Johnny had on a blue pinafore!"

"That must be Charley Jones!" said Letty, who, with little Sally in her arms, had strolled up to the castle just to look about her, Mima and Rachel having brought down word that it was the easiest thing in the world to go there, and the most amusing. "It's Charley Jones—I know it is!" said Letty; "whatever will his mother say?" and then she sate down and cried, for it was a sad sight, and enough to melt a heart much harder than hers. She did not stop to look at any of the wonders of the ruins, but, taking little Sally again in her arms, made the best of her way to Mrs. Jones's. Mrs. Jones was by this time quite sober, and sadly out of spirits likewise, by the excesses of the former days and nights. She set up a loud lamentation when she heard Letty's tidings, and, wringing her hands and crying bitterly as she went, she found that indeed it was Charley—her own favourite Charley—who lay there on the ground, mangled and blackened, and who had found his death, in some measure, by her own hands; for she herself had snatched up a torch, and, rushing into the castle the first moment the doors were broken open, had been one of the first to set fire to it.

One by one, the leaders and agents in this violent

and sudden outbreak shrunk back to their various
homes or hiding-places, accordingly as they considered
themselves amenable to justice. Three days after the
castle was burnt, constables came to Ford's house to
apprehend him as one of the principal instigators; but
he was not there—he had not yet made his appearance
at home.

The new Mrs. Ford made loud lamentations on what
she called her bereaved state; and the next week
Mr. Bartram distrained again for the rent due, giving
them also notice immediately to quit, saying, he would
wash his hands at once of such disgraceful tenants.
A fresh home was accordingly sought out; and, in a
day or two, the former Mrs. Higgins removed, with her
two daughters and two step-daughters, and the miserable remains of the Fords' once goodly possessions, to
a new habitation.

Soon after this, something very unpleasant occurred
between Mima and her employer; what it was, however, was not told to Letty. Her mother was furiously
angry, and threatened to turn her out of doors; upon
which Mima sate and cried for three days in her bedroom. Rachel went to work, as usual, at the warehouse; and, having quarrelled with Mima, became
kinder to Letty. She would sit and nurse little Sally,
and kiss her and cry over her. Sometimes she used to
talk of going out to service, and sometimes, of putting
herself apprentice to a dressmaker; "anything," she
said, "she would do, rather than remain at home, with
things as they then were."

Letty had never seen Mrs. Greaseley since she left
their lodgings; nobody could tell her where they lived,
although she had inquired from every one to whom she
dared mention the name. She was coming, one afternoon, from the Ruben's Head, where she had been
with a private message to Jane, informing her that her
father was safe, nor need she be apprehensive about
him, when she was overjoyed, although she trembled

exceedingly, by meeting Mrs. Greaseley. The dear
old woman looked just as usual—so neat and so clean,
in her snuff-coloured bombazine, red cloak, and little
black bonnet. She seemed quite delighted to meet
Letty.

"Where do you live now, child?" said she: "I've
been into Bartram's Court to find you, and could not.
You must go home with me; for my asthma is bad; I
cannot stand talking here, and I have a deal to say to
you."

Letty never thought about her being wanted at
home, nor about little Sally; but, only too grateful,
too happy to be so invited, turned back with the old
woman, who took her hand into hers, just as she used
to do when they went to church together. If Letty
had been in heaven she could not have been happier,
although she felt a choking sensation in her throat
that made her rather uncomfortable. "I've something to say to you very particular, Letty," said Mrs.
Greaseley, "but I'll say it when I'm at home; that'll
be better, Letty, won't it?" Letty said "Yes," for
she was too happy to be impatient.

They walked on till they came to the Mansfield
Road, and then into a pretty little house, where a
widow lived who was a dress-maker, and so into a
little parlour, with a carpet on the floor, and where the
furniture stood just as it used to do in their upper
room, only looking, Letty thought, a great deal nicer.
Letty turned her eyes away from the little walnut-tree
box, for someway she felt ashamed and troubled at
the sight of it. The little round tea-tray stood on the
table, ready for tea, and the kettle was singing on
the fire. Mrs. Greaseley made Letty sit down, and
then, taking out her keys, reached from a cupboard
another cup and saucer and the bread and butter.

"I would have had a bit of cake," said Mrs. Greaseley, "if I'd thought of having you to tea, child."

"Oh, dear!" said Letty, getting up from her chair,

and unable longer to remain silent, "do tell me have you forgiven me, and do you believe I never stole the money? if so, I want nothing else!"

"Yes," returned Mrs. Greaseley, "I do believe it. I do believe you a good girl; and you've been badly used, Letty, that you have! Oh, child, I haven't been able to sleep for nights for thinking of you—and it troubled me so that I couldn't find you. 'You must find her,' says my master (for I told him all;) 'you must let her know,' says he, 'that she's clear—that's no more than justice.'"

Poor Letty leaned forward to the table, and drank in these words with unspeakable joy. "Take your tea, Letty," said Mrs. Greaseley, who had poured out a cup which remained untouched; "drink your tea, child, for I've made it very good."

"I never was so happy in all my life," said the girl, drinking her tea, but never thinking whether it was good or bad. Presently the old woman got up, and, unlocking the little walnut-tree box, took out the old-fashioned gold-brocade housewife, which she put into Letty's hand—"It's safe, you see," said she.

"Where did you find it?" exclaimed Letty, with the utmost delight of look and tone; "and have you found the money?"

"You shall keep that housewife now!" said Mrs. Greaseley; "I always meant to have left it to you when I died; but I give it you now—you deserve it! Poor thing!" added she, in a tone of the kindest sympathy, "you deserve it—that you do! I will confess, Letty," said she, "that I'm very fond of you; and, if it were not for the old man, you should come and live with me—that you should!"

Letty seized the old woman's hand, and kissed it and wetted it with tears.

"I'll tell you, child," said Mrs. Greaseley, after a moment or two, "how I found it out. I wanted a fire-shovel and two or three odd things, which Mrs.

Q

Green, my landlady, advised me to get at a pawn-broker's sale of pledges. It was last Friday I went to a pawnbroker's in the Market-place. I didn't get what I wanted, however, for they were selling watches and fancy articles. I was just coming away, when what should I see but my little housewife! I knew it in a minute, and bid for it—I got it for eightpence; had it been eight shillings I think I should have paid it, I set such store by it; and, besides, I thought directly I should get at the truth through it. The next day I went to the pawnbroker's, and asked who had pledged it. He said, right and clear at once, one Jemima Higgins." Letty started, and her face became first pale and then crimson, for it was terrible to have her suspicion of her sister thus verified. " I remembered what you had said, Letty," continued her friend; " but I said nothing to the pawnbroker: there was a man, however, standing at that moment by the counter, and ' Jemima Higgins!' says he, ' she's a bad 'un; it's only last week,' says he, ' that she was found carrying off a piece of net from Warrington's, where she worked; they are shocking bad people, all the family; the step-father has got into trouble about the Castle-burning and the riots—they'll hang him if they find him.' That was the first word, Letty, said Mrs. Grease-ley, "that I had heard about your mother having married Mr. Ford. Lord! how surprised I was. Why, it's enough to make the first Mrs. Ford come out of her grave!"

" Oh, dear!" said Letty, " is it not shocking? but I don't think they'll find him—and I'm sure I hope they won't, if it's only for little Sally's sake! You never saw little Sally, did you?" Letty had a deal to tell her friend, before she made her thoroughly acquainted with all the sad and strange events that had happened since she left; and every now and then she interrupted herself, to give vent to her joy, or to speak out some thought which was a digression.—" Oh, dear! how could anybody think I should rob you?—don't you remember the pretty gown you gave me? and do you know," said she, "I never made it up—I hardly had the heart ever to look at it since, it made me cry so when I did! I meant to keep it for years and years, and make it up for little Sally when I took her with me to church."

"Well, Letty, I'll tell you what you shall do," said Mrs. Greaseley; "you shall bring it here to-morrow, and come and stop all day with me; and bring little Sally with you; and I'll have a bit of mutton with potatoes under it, and a rice pudding, to dinner; and Mrs. Green shall help us to make it. We'll have a nice day together, Letty, won't we?"

"I don't think this is a dream," said Letty; "but, dear me, it seems almost like one!"

———

All that winter, and till the next spring assizes, Ford was obliged to keep in hiding. Various were his places of concealment, and most severe were his sufferings both of body and mind; but fear of the vengeance of the law was stronger than all; and, in sickness and want and sorrow, the winter went wearily by. The assizes came at length. His associates were tried, and three of them condemned to death, among whom was Mima's friend, Mr. Curly Hearson. Mima compassed, by some means or other, a suit of mourning; and, having received a farewell letter and a pockethandkerchief as a keepsake from the unhappy man, three days before his execution, she bewailed his loss— for the time at least—with sincere sorrow.

THE END.

CPSIA information can be obtained at www.ICGtesting.com
Printed in the USA
BVOW02s1035310815

415867BV00027B/725/P